STOP BEING YOUR OWN WORST ENEMY!

By

Jagat Viradia

"Connect the Vision"
Nexus Stories Publication
Bharata

NEXUS STORIES PUBLICATION®
Surat, Gujarat, India.

Title – **Stop Being Your Own Worst Enemy!**
First Published by Nexus Stories Publication 2025

ISBN # 978-81-972524-9-5

Contributor: Sakshi Viradia

Publication
Nexus Stories Publication®, Surat (Gujarat), Bhārata
www.nexus-stories.com | +91 87800 80718

Dedication

I dedicate this book to You.

Because you are the one who completes the circle. A circle that began with my experiences. All the lessons I learned. And I am happy to share with you through this book.

This book is small in the first draft, and it will grow with your input in the time to come. This is the first step in self-growth that I created for myself. And my brother pushed me to publish it. I am thankful to all my friends and family for providing me with the environment and, yes, the experiences!

Now that you are going to read this book, name it your book. Write your reflection on the ideas I have shared here.

Introduction

Hi, I am Jagat. And this is my first book. Of course, I am not fully ready to publish a book. But then there is no tomorrow. And a perfect book is a mirage like everything else. I decided to take the first step. And learn as I make my way.

I have been a very average person. I used to prefer standing behind a crowd so that people wouldn't find out my level of dumbness. The past few years were different. It is a bit funny. You might find it interesting. Due to many reasons, my digestion improved. Yes. And that made my head function differently. And I found my fear to be a friend. Always over-protecting me.

I restarted learning all my favorite subjects, and I began with "Learning how to learn!". And that improved my reading and writing. This made me think that I could jump the hurdles and friction of opposing forces within myself. How? This book explains.

I reached a point of sufficient clarity. The realization that deep down there is no negative or positive. It is one whole. An UNDIVIDED unicity. Say, non-duality. This book is my sincere and joyous attempt to point out that you belong to a higher trajectory. Godspeed.

Jagat Viradia

Date: 3 Dec 2022 # Surat.

Prologue

Everything we see around us teaches us, programs us, or conditions us to become who we are. Zoom out and see the big picture. You may wake up to a hidden reality. The one that you call your "self" is a minority in the cluster that is "you". Yes, inside you there is very little actual you. The show is running on its own, and you think you are an “in-dividual”. (I’ll share as you read further why I hyphened to divide the “in” and “dividual”.)

It is a fact that you are a cluster of so many moving parts. Call it many minds, many personalities, masks. There is a constant war going on within you. This conflict is within parts of your mind that are rarely in harmony, well almost never!

This book may feel a little hard to go through as your inner system will resist absorbing the ideas. Relax, you are stronger than that. And yes, this book will get you the missing pieces that you have been searching for. And one more thing, you are born free. Let your mind change as you upgrade your thinking.

Let go of your fixed ideas and look at everything with fresh eyes. Think again. As a matter of fact, even the way you are sitting too needs thinking again. Sit straight! ;-)

Foreword

Okay, get this... Fear is your friend. I know it's hard to believe, but then again, why would you feel this emotion in the first place if it wasn't your friend, right?

I often had this discussion with my dad. And we came to the conclusion, that this idea opens the gates to many answers. Be it sports, socializing, or doing something extraordinary. Repeat this mantra, "Fear is a friend", and then everything will start to make sense.

This idea inspired me. And right then I got an invitation to give a TEDx talk. I gave it an interesting title. "A friend called Mind. Do you mind?"

Since then, we have been discussing this idea. The idea is simple. All such important emotions have had bad publicity. Deep down, they are our true friends and always try to protect us. We thought of creating a small book around this idea.

I am happy to to contribute my active inputs, a whole chapter and a lot of conversation on the ideas behind this book.

Sakshi Viradia

Acknowledgment

It has been a long journey. A journey to create my own time management system. Sounds boring, yeah. But this time it is different! A system to manage time, energy, attention, and all that I have. So that I can invest all my resources in growth. An understanding that helps me find peace and satisfaction in everyday life.

I am happy to announce that I have arrived at a lush green plateau and now going further. My brother Niraj already shared with his network that Jagat is working on a book. I had written a few pages and was thinking about how to make it simple so that you enjoy reading and more. I am very secretive about my inner world, you know... and I wasn't too keen to go public, but then I thought about it again and here I am.

Furthermore, I often thought of going to the past to meet my teenage self. Just so that I can pass on helpful ideas. I share such ideas with my daughter. Her feedback is part of my writing.

Announcing the book pushed me to focus and create a piece of my learning in the form of a book without delay. You should try that for your projects. ;-)

Jagat Viradia

Index

_Toc190929976

1
NOTE TO THE READER

This book is an open and ongoing project. See it as a living book, like a living person that has the potential to grow. Together we will see it grow as you read, page by page. Because when you read, you may come up with interesting questions. Questions based on your life and experiences. Your problems and your experiments to find solutions.

I invite you to be a part of this book project. Send your words on my Twitter. We will have conversations over live sessions on Instagram. We can interact on my YouTube channel. Probably a little boring for you, but yes, You can also write to me at length at jagatviradia@gmail.com.

Together, our inputs will enrich this book.

I will keep updating this book. Your suggestions, advice, and questions are important to me. I wish to include your voice along with my responses in future updates of this book. Do specify if you want me to mention your name or keep it hidden!

2
BEFORE SELF-HELP

We read self-help books fondly. Every time a new self-help book is in our hands, we feel hopeful. Because we want to transform ourselves into something better. Our standard for this something "imaginary" better comes from what we have seen in other people.

For self-help, the first thing we need is clarity on what "self" is. Generally, you think of yourself as a single individual. Let's break it down and see what an individual contains.

An individual in Sanskrit is called "Purusha". And a city is called "Pur". You are not one but a whole city inside your head. Many people live inside your mind. They are all different parts of your mind.

Each one is like an individual program. And each program is interacting with all the other programs. This creates a complex web full of interesting combinations.

Everything that happens in a city is happening in your mind. There are all possible genders with different ages and colors and tastes. Just like people in a town, there are inner splits and different types of relationships.

There are friends and there are foes. There is temporary dating and there are couples tightly bonded. Jealousy and competition between parts are the norms.

It is all divided, and every part has an opinion. There is competition and jealousy and love and friendship and everything we know and beyond.

"You are a city. Purusha is made of Pur. It is full of variety. Sometimes there is chaos and sometimes celebration. To understand yourself, you have to meet each citizen of your inner city with openness."

In your waking hours, you put a lot of effort to keep the law and order. And still, at times, you lose control. When you are asleep, the inner city behaves differently. This is the time when the city is free from your interventions and goes into its own drama called dreams.

Any new self-help idea is like a new citizen entering your inner city. This newcomer has to find its true place within this largely populated place. Sounds difficult, right? Because it is.

By now, it should start to make sense why all those self-help books are not that effective practically. The first prerequisite is to prepare the inner city. After that, the acceptance of a new idea will begin to take effect.

This is how nature has designed the system. And we have got to begin to work with what we have in the present. It is an interesting challenge and a kinda puzzle to solve.

You look for self-help ideas to change yourself. Why?
Let us find out.

"You are a City"

Exercises:

1. Dream Journal: Keep a journal by your bedside to record your dreams regularly. Reflect on these entries and look for recurring themes, characters, or scenarios. Consider how these dream elements might relate to the dynamics within your inner city.

2. Mindful Observation: Throughout the day, practice mindful observation of your thoughts and emotions. Take note of any conflicts, alliances, or patterns in your mental landscape. Consider keeping a daily log to track your observations.

3. Open Dialogue: Choose a quiet moment to engage in an imaginary open dialogue with one of the citizens of your inner city. Write a conversation where you explore their perspectives, opinions, and desires. This can provide insights into different aspects of your mindset.

Questions to Ponder:

1. Inner City Reflection: How does the concept of viewing yourself as an inner city with various citizens change or enhance your understanding of your own complexity?

2. Citizen Harmony: Reflect on the citizens within your inner city. Are they in harmony, or do you observe conflicts and tensions? How might these dynamics impact your overall mindset and actions?

3. Dream Analysis: After maintaining a dream journal for some time, what patterns or insights emerge? How do these dream elements correlate with your waking life experiences and inner city dynamics?

4. Openness to Exploration: Assess your current level of openness to exploring different aspects of your own mind. Are there specific citizens or parts you tend to avoid or resist understanding? How might increasing openness contribute to personal growth?

5. Self-Help Motivation: Revisit your motivations for seeking self-help ideas. Are you driven more by a desire to conform to external standards, or do you genuinely seek personal growth for intrinsic reasons? How might aligning your motivations impact the effectiveness of self-help practices?

3.
YOUR OPERATING SYSTEM

Every city has a method of governance. There are certain soft rules and etiquette. Then there are strict laws. Codes of conduct and SOPs. There are written laws and unwritten understandings. Every citizen follows it and that is how the city runs smoothly. You know what happens when there are riots and civil unrest. It takes a good doze of sanity and strictness to bring the city back to normal.

This model is a good thought experiment for an individual "Purusha". Inside you, there is a city. Analyze it from this point of view.

How do you operate inside your inner world, your mind? Do you take opinions of all the parts of your mind?

Are you democratic? Do you go with the majority of your mind and the opposing part supports once a decision is made?

Or is it a tribal setup? The part that opposes a decision comes back later to give you loads of guilt if things go bad.

Some of us are autocratic. They have strict laws for themselves. Everything that comes up as grievances is put aside or put into a deep and dark prison of the subconscious. There is a possibility of revolt. Maybe in the form of physical or mental illness!

A meeting with self is an open-door brainstorming with the entire group of citizens. A festival of higher thinking with respect and warmth to all the parts of the mind. A meeting to plan new adventures and explorations.

"Inner democracy within your mind brings the best talent to the forefront."

- To filter out any foreign idea taken in at face value.
- To keep what is original and think independently.
- To carve out long-term beneficial ideas and discard the short-term escapes.
- To understand addictions and their root cause.
- To heal and repair.
- To add new routines for expansion.

There is a good chance of finding and keeping worthwhile learning from the experiences.

There are certain decisions, that you regret later on. Do you know why? Because you did not have a meeting with all the mind citizens and took their opinions. It was a hasty decision, like a sudden reflex. Only a part of your mind was involved. Later, when the remaining parts got involved, the decision appeared faulty. Now, altering many such decisions may or may not be possible.

The best you can do with this is to reflect on that episode and relive it to absorb the learning. Try a thought experiment. See what was possible if things were handled differently and with a **Stop Being Your Own Worst Enemy!** Imagine, if this becomes your operating system. A democratic and friendly environment inside. The world outside will look a much better place.

Exercises:

1. Decision-Making Styles Quiz: Develop a quiz to identify your predominant decision-making style within your inner city. Include questions that assess if your approach is democratic, tribal, autocratic, or a combination of these. Reflect on the results to understand your current mindset.
2. Inner City Council Meeting: Set aside dedicated time for an imaginary council meeting with the citizens of your inner city. Write a script or journal entry detailing how different parts express their opinions on a specific decision or challenge. Consider the dynamics and resolutions reached.
3. Exploration Routine: Introduce a new routine for exploration within your inner city. This could be a daily reflection, meditation, or journaling session where you

actively engage with different citizens, seeking their opinions and insights on various aspects of your life.

Questions to Ponder:

1. Governance Reflection: Upon creating a sketch of your inner city's governance system, what insights did you gain about the dynamics and decision-making processes within your mind? Are there parts that play dominant roles, and how does this influence your mindset?
2. Exploration Routine Impact: If you introduced a new routine for exploration within your inner city, how has it impacted your mindset and motivation for self-growth? Have you noticed any changes in your awareness of different aspects of your mind?
3. Parallel Reality Insights: Consider the parallel reality scenario where your inner city operates democratically and with friendliness. What insights did you gain from this exploration, and how might incorporating elements of this alternative operating system positively affect your interactions with the external world?
4. Regretful Decisions Reflection: Reflect on decisions that you later regretted. Were these decisions made impulsively, with only a part of your mind involved? How might involving all citizens in your inner city influence future decision-making and reduce the likelihood of regret?
5. Learning from Mistakes: Explore the idea of reliving episodes of regret to absorb the learning. How can this practice contribute to your self-growth and development of a **Stop Being Your Own Worst Enemy!** Are there specific patterns or lessons that emerge from such reflections?

4.
WHY SELF-HELP

This idea of change in self comes to you from somewhere. You may falsely assume it to be our own creation. In the language of machines, you want to create the next version of yourself. There are two possible scenarios.

We went through the idea of the inner city. The majority of people inside the city have this wish, and therefore it comes to the surface. There are many such wishes, but the majority is not clear about them, and therefore it is not visible. You can say, those ideas are in the subconscious mind.

Scenario 1. You want to change because you are fed up with your present state of mind-body. You want a revolution. Not only that, but you want to break apart the city and create a better one.

Scenario 2. You are happy with the present state and out of love for your inner city, you wish to upgrade it. You wish to enhance and improve the city. Furthermore, you want to upgrade and expand.

These are two completely different scenarios. And the consequences of each will be very different. Why? Because what you are going to create will have the entire population of your inner city in it. If these citizens are not in harmony, all new developments will return to the same old state.

"If your desire to transform the self is out of love for your mind-body, your inner city, the upgrade will flourish."

So the question is, how to bring harmony to multicultural citizens in the inner city?

Theoretically, it is simple. By meeting each citizen and making friends. Sounds difficult? Well, it is. There are many whom you will not even recognize. There are many hidden ones. The reason they were hiding is that you disapprove of them because of societal conditioning. Inherently, they are beautiful parts with special capabilities and uniqueness. This is generally not accepted in society. So you disowned them and they went in underground.

Practically, it is a continuous process of welcoming each part of your mind, your inner citizen, to surface and become visible. Accept it warmly as your part. Give it respect and listen to what this part has to say. And this dialogue remains continuous for the rest of your life. It is a rich hangout of all citizens finding ways to create a harmony of friendship. There is nothing more beautiful than a person uniting within and becoming truly UNDIVIDED.

Exercises:

1. Scenario Reflection: Reflect on the two scenarios presented—wanting a revolution or desiring an upgrade. Write down specific instances or feelings that align with each scenario in your life. Consider which scenario resonates more with your present mindset and motivation for self-growth.

2. Citizen Recognition Exercise: List various citizens or parts within your inner city that you recognize and appreciate. Then, explore hidden or disowned citizens that may need acknowledgment. Write a letter of acceptance to one of these hidden citizens, expressing your willingness to understand and appreciate them.

3. Continuous Dialogue Journal: Start a journal dedicated to the continuous dialogue with different citizens of your

inner city. Record your thoughts, feelings, and interactions with various parts. Use this journal as a tool for ongoing self-reflection and building harmony within.

Questions to Ponder:

1. Inner City Harmony Reflection: After creating the Inner City Harmony Map, what insights did you gain about the current state of harmony within your inner city? Are there specific citizens or parts that seem to be in discord, and how does this reflect in your daily life?

2. Scenario Alignment: Reflect on the presented scenarios of wanting a revolution or desiring an upgrade. Which scenario resonates more with your current mindset and motivation for self-growth? Can you identify specific instances in your life that align with one of these scenarios?

3. Hidden Citizen Acknowledgment: Through the Citizen Recognition Exercise, did you discover any hidden or disowned citizens within your inner city? How willing are you to acknowledge and embrace these parts? What societal conditioning might have led to their hiding?

4. Personal Hangout of Unity: Envision a future where your inner city is truly united and undivided. How does this affect your overall well-being, decision-making, and interactions with the external world? What specific actions can you take to create a rich hangout of unity within?

5. ABOUT: CONTRACT WITH SELF

So this one is a biggie. After a lot of stumbling and falling, I have reached this clarity. A point where I can make you find that hidden door to everything and anything you want to achieve. One name for that is "a contract with self".

Why

Let's say you have a list of things you want to do during the day. Firstly, that is a good try. But then the reality hits. At the end of your day, looking back to how the day went is not a happy picture. Why? Because your mind made you drop off the train and wander sideways.

It took me a long time to realize that I need a better strategy. No matter how much I push down the unimportant things, they always find their way in. This looks almost like some kind of leakage in a restricted system.

So I played with this idea of an inverse model of thinking. And I thought to try and focus on the unimportant things first. Yeah, I know it sounds strange. But this worked. By giving unimportant things a proper time slot. I also made sure not to carry any guilt afterward. In the beginning, I did not force myself to do any of the important things. I let myself relax during this experiment to observe what happens.

"Learn to accept the state of being where no chaos is present."

A point came when I found after doing the unimportant things I had no guilt. My mind was quiet and ready and eager to take up the important activities. I thought it might be a one-time thing. But I did many experiments. And it worked, every time!

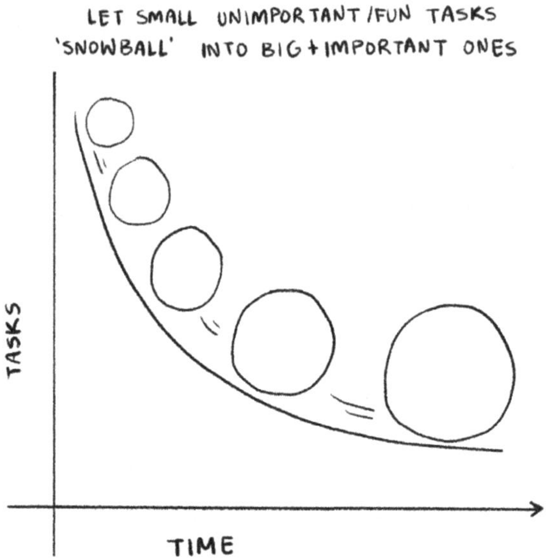

Now that was not expected. Because usually, we are expecting constant struggle within. And when the struggle is not there, you feel awkward. Yes, it is strange, but we are so used to living in chaos. Change requires courage and a fresh perspective.

How

I make a contract with myself every day for the next 24 hours. This contract starts with unimportant but fun activities. All my habits/needs attract me and are always on my mind. And they pull me, especially at times When I am doing something very important. I give them a proper time slot and I also invite the mood of those things at its time.

This made my mind quiet. Why? Because i gave my mind assurance. My mind does not have to struggle anymore. It doesn't need to find sneaky ways to divert me from those activities. This stopped the leakage of energy. Now I have given a structure to my mind. This structure gives me a clean and uninterrupted productive space. And in this space, I move like a sprinter into all the important activities that I want to do.

The next on the list are the important activities of the day. Here, if need be, list down the 2nd and 3rd options for important activities. This will keep the flow going in case I am not in the mood for option 1. I can still use the creative energy to explore other options and drift away, wasting my time. Even the little to-do should be there at its proper time. There can be random activities on a side column.

What

Now, when I am doing important and productive activities, my mind is one hundred percent into it. Because all the not urgent and important activities are waiting for their time slots. And even if the urge arises to jump onto those activities, the mind becomes a kind of auto-answering machine. It reminds itself that there is a proper time slot already assigned. So take a step back! And I return to my flow.

I extended this idea to think with focus. There are many thoughts floating in my mind. When I write them down and give them a proper time slot for focused thinking, then stop to float. And I found that the mind feels like seeing through the clear water.
Now that I have designed and devised this strategy and put it into action, it made me think wider.

So I zoom out to look at the big picture. I realize that the state of chaos and confusion and fogginess was my unconscious choice. And it kind of protected me from confronting actual life as it unfolds. And that happened because I was running out of tools to handle life situations better. Keeping myself in a confused state gave me less guilt for not being able to handle life the way it should. But I realized that it is a disease and needs repairing. all this for growth as fast as possible. And making an all-inclusive contract with self is the way. It is like a peace treaty with the inner forces. These forces are generally divided and are enemies of one another. This situation used to keep my system in turbulence and in an inner conflict mode all the time.

Buddha once said: If you win yourself, you win the world!

I am sure you're ready for more. So put on your diving gears and let's dive in and go deeper to find out more.

Exercises:

1. Daily Contract Design: Create a daily contract with yourself, outlining specific time slots for both unimportant but fun activities and important tasks. Design a visual representation of this contract, making it a tangible reminder throughout the day. Reflect on how this structured approach impacts your mindset and productivity.
2. Unimportant Activity Awareness: Spend a day consciously observing and noting unimportant but fun activities that usually distract you. How often do these activities enter your thoughts? Analyze their patterns and identify time slots in your daily routine to accommodate them, as suggested in the text.
3. Focused Thinking Time Slots: Experiment with allocating specific time slots for focused thinking on various thoughts that float in your mind. Jot down these thoughts and designate dedicated periods for contemplation. Reflect on how this practice influences your clarity of thinking and overall mental state.

4. Big Picture Reflection: Zoom out and reflect on the big picture of your life before and after implementing the daily contract strategy. How has your mindset shifted? What changes have you observed in your ability to handle life situations and confront challenges? Consider documenting these insights in a journal.

Questions to Ponder:

1. Unimportant Activity Impact: How do unimportant but fun activities typically impact your daily productivity and mindset? Can you recall instances where these activities diverted your attention from important tasks?
2. Structured Mind Reflection: After designing and implementing the daily contract, reflect on how the structured flow of your mind influences your day. Do you find it easier to stay focused on important tasks? How does this structure impact your overall mental state?
3. Chaos as an Unconscious Choice: Reflect on the notion that chaos, confusion, and fogginess might have been an unconscious choice. Do you resonate with this idea? In what ways did maintaining a confused state serve as a protective mechanism, and what realizations does this bring?
4. Peace Treaty with Inner Forces: Consider the concept of making a peace treaty with your inner forces through an all-inclusive contract. How do you perceive the different inner forces within you? In what ways can a structured contract serve as a peace treaty, resolving inner conflicts and promoting growth?

START WITH THE WHY

6.
MODEL OF ENERGY ATTENTION & TIMEȦ

Imagine if you have a piece of land, a farm. This farm's name is Time. There is a water tank on the farm. This tank has Energy inside it. There is a pipe that carries the energy to the farm. This pipe is Attention.

What if I tell you that our precious pipe is punctured? How? Because it is old and has many holes made by the world around you. The water will not reach up to where you want it to. The water is getting wasted and weeds are growing everywhere. Sounds familiar?

Now, it is not all your fault that the pipe got holes everywhere and caused it to leak. There are so many pokers all around us wanting free water. They are looking for even the faintest opportunity to poke a hole or two in the pipe and steal the precious water.

Funny thing is, you don't know this interesting fact. The surrounding environment is training to enjoy this leakage of energy. And most times, you are allowing the pokers to poke the hole in your vital energy pipe. Sadistic pleasure! The biggest energy drain today is mobile phones. And this lineup includes all such bright and colorful screens and electronics. Don't take me wrong. I am an electronics engineer myself, and I am fascinated by all new technology things. Technology must be under our command. And not the reverse!

Now, the action items are as follows.

"It is like gardening skill. Giving the right amount of water to the right area through a leakproof and flexible pipe!"

Protect your pipe. Plan how you want to channel the water. The specific time and specific area.

And then there will be moments when you just feel like blowing away the water in a frenzy of a blast.. Yeah, why not! It will be pure joy when it is your conscious decision. All I am saying is that it better not be a raid from the outsiders. Watch out for raids trying to break your pipe and steal the water and leaving you empty, barren and _________! (Fill your own word in the blank space ;-)

Always remember. Plan before you begin your trip. You will save a lot of energy and will be in command to invest the energy where it has the potential to grow multifold. This will be a rewarding process. The one that builds you up to be stronger and clearer.

Exercises:

1. Mobile Phone Audit: Conduct a detailed audit of your mobile phone usage. Track the time spent on different apps and activities. Identify which activities contribute positively to your well-being and growth and which ones act as energy drains. Consider creating a plan to manage and optimize your phone usage.

2. Raid Prevention Strategy: Reflect on instances where external factors (raids) might have negatively influenced your energy pipe. Develop a strategy to prevent such raids, whether they come in the form of distractions, external pressures, or societal expectations. Consider how proactive measures can safeguard your energy.

3. Trip Planning Analogy: Extend the analogy of planning before a trip to your daily activities. Before starting your day, create a mental or written plan outlining how you intend to allocate your energy and attention. Reflect on how this planning approach enhances your ability to stay focused and invest energy where it truly matters.

Questions to Ponder:

1. Awareness of Energy Drains: How aware are you of potential energy drains in your daily life, especially those caused by external factors like mobile phones or societal pressures? Reflect on specific instances where you felt your energy leaking away.

2. Metaphor Personalization: In the context of the farm metaphor, how would you personalize your own farm? What areas of your life represent different sections of the farm, and where would you intentionally channel your energy for growth?

3. Reflection on Raids: Have you experienced "raids" on your energy pipe from external influences? Identify these influences and reflect on how they impacted your energy levels and overall well-being.

4. Intentional Watering Plan: Consider the concept of intentional watering in your life. What specific plans can you implement to protect your energy pipe and channel water (energy) to areas that align with your personal and growth-oriented goals?

5. Proactive Trip Planning: How does the analogy of planning before a trip resonate with your daily activities? Reflect on the effectiveness of planning your day in advance to save energy and invest it in areas that contribute to your personal development and growth.

7.
BUILDING DAMS AND CANALS

Building a dam and canals for your river of time, energy, and attention. I like history. In parts where I don't have to remember the dates! In the old times and partly even today, the rivers used to run wild and would flood every few years. This is how it used to be since the first man stood on the ground.

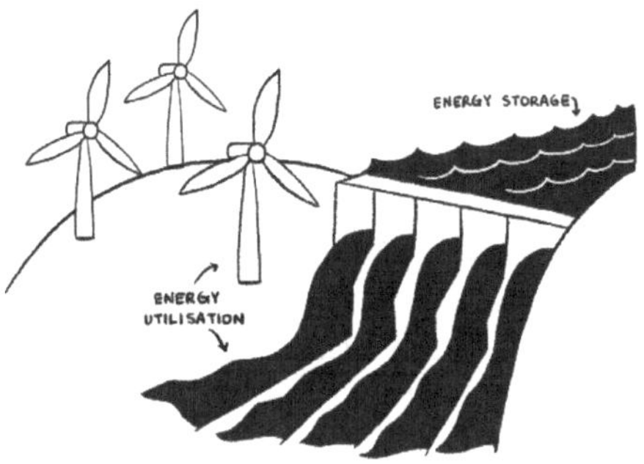

And the revolution began in recent times when we engineered ways to build dams and tame the wild rivers. The canals bring the water in a controlled way to where we need the most. The rising population got the crops and food it needed, and it made the world a better place for so many of us. Also, we learned to generate electricity from the power of water.

This should switch on a light bulb in our head, saying that we too are sources of energy. (Well, not when you stretch out on a couch. And don't want to move a step away even if that remote is 3 inches away from your reach. Strange as $#%@, not?) And most of us are unaware. Unaware that the energy is flowing away into useless activities. We are being robbed of our precious inner resources. Big words, ha? But you get the scene.

"In short, you must realize that energy can be put into use and planned action. First, save the energy and then invest with clear intentions and focus."

You need to design your own dam and canals. Then the resources will flow where YOU decide. This will be a productive and guilt-free journey once the system is up and running.

This idea may have never struck you before, and I deserve the credit B-). Well, simply saying, waking up to this is a big step and working on it is the next one. Contract with self (CWS) is a system I am going to share in the upcoming pages to build you up from the inside out.
Now, if you're still reading, give me a nod. Thanks. I got a plan. Stick with me, and it will all work out well.

Exercises:

1. Design Your Dam: Metaphorically design your own dam to control the flow of energy and attention. Identify specific areas in your life where you want to build these dams to prevent energy leakage. Consider what tools or strategies you need to construct and maintain these dams effectively.

2. Reflection on Inner Resources: Reflect on the concept of being a source of energy. Identify moments or situations in your daily life where you feel your energy is not utilized effectively. Consider how implementing dams and canals could enhance the preservation and utilization of your inner resources.

Questions to Ponder:

1. Awareness of Energy Flow: How aware are you of the flow of your time, energy, and attention in your daily life? Reflect on moments when you feel these resources are flowing freely and moments when they might be getting wasted.

2. Recognition of Energy Robbery: Can you identify specific activities or situations that might be robbing you of energy? How does this awareness impact your mindset, and what steps can you take to minimize energy robbery?

3. Imagining Your Dams: If you were to build dams in your life, where would you place them? Consider both external factors (distractions, external pressures) and internal factors (negative thought patterns, unproductive habits). How might building these dams improve your overall well-being?

4. Intentional Canals: Where would you construct intentional canals to direct your energy towards meaningful activities? Identify key areas in your life where intentional channels could lead to increased productivity and personal growth.

5. Personal Commitment: How committed are you to designing your own dams and canals to control and direct your energy? Consider the level of motivation and determination you have to implement changes in the flow of your inner resources.

8.
BAD HABIT : AN INTERESTING MODEL!

Except you're a secretive saint claiming to have no bad habits, you're like me. I mean, of course, you're unique with some unique bad habits. My point is, just observe the bad habits carefully. You'll inevitably come to the realization that there is a lot to learn from it.

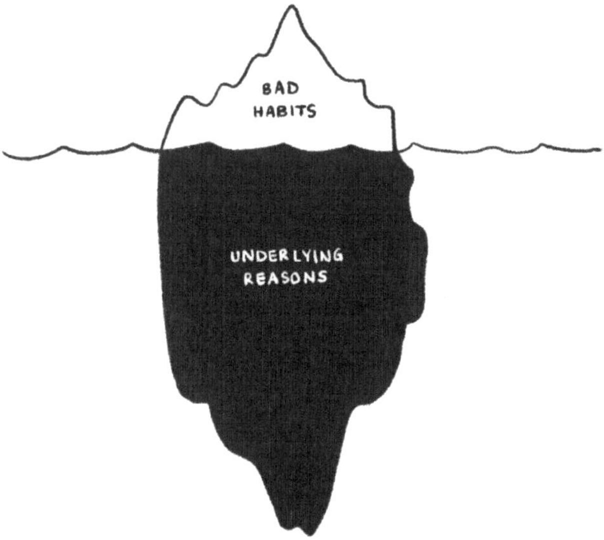

You did it once, a long, long time ago. Maybe it was not such a great experience. Remember? But, eventually, your system pulled you into it in spite of your surface reluctance. Yes, surface. You went into it again because one living inside you wanted to do it again.

There's an important lesson here. Deep down, you get some joy out of it. Even if it is for a few moments. It satisfies some hidden craving. Also, it has the power to distract you from everything else for that period of time. All good. But then there's also a thing called guilt. It comes right behind it, even if you accept it or not.

Remember, guilt isn't your original product. You got it from people around and the whole world outside. Imagine if you were the only person on this planet, there was nothing like guilt in your life. People try to teach us the good and bad. It has the functional purpose to steer through life most of the time. But if you accept it as some kind of writing on the stone, it will weigh you down. And You already know this, right?

Think. You have not created guilt. It is almost an automatic process of the brain. Because brain programming is usually the work of the society. And guess what, you can reprogram it. Simple. Well, ok it's not so simple but step by step surely you can overcome it.

"Bad habits are like icebergs. The visible part of invisible reasons beneath. To discover the reasons, the First step is to drop the guilt."

Acceptance of this side of your nature will make you a little more wholesome. And let me tell you a secret. Once you accept this dark side in you, it no more remains as dark as it used to be. There will be a natural and organic change. No. Don't get ahead of yourself. The change will be unique for you. Yes, understanding will certainly deepen.

Maybe, the bad habit will no more appear as bad as it used to be. Maybe the intensity will soften, and maybe the habit could drop away, who knows!

Bad habits enter to fill a certain unknown gap in our being. Forcibly rejecting it will only make it intense. It is like something is knocking on your door, and you are trying to hold the door (Hodor.. Hodor..). After a point you get tired and the habit breaks in. A lot of energy is wasted. This isn't smart. Let it come in and be friends with it. Talk to it. Find out why is it there.

Exercises:

1. Habit Observation Journal: Create a habit observation journal. List down one or two bad habits you want to understand better. For each habit, document the circumstances, emotions, and thoughts associated with engaging in the habit. This can help you identify patterns and triggers.
2. Root Cause Reflection: Reflect on the root cause of a specific bad habit. Consider the emotions or situations that lead to the habit. Write a short narrative exploring the deeper reasons behind the habit. This exercise aims to bring awareness to the hidden aspects of your behavior.
3. Guilt Release Practice: Develop a ritual or practice to release guilt associated with a particular bad habit. This could involve writing down the guilt on paper and then tearing it apart or using visualization techniques to let go of guilt. Reflect on how this practice affects your mindset.
4. Reprogramming Brain Patterns: Identify societal or external influences that contributed to feelings of guilt associated with your bad habits. Counteract these influences by consciously reprogramming your mindset. Write down positive affirmations or alternative beliefs that challenge guilt-inducing thoughts.
5. Acceptance and Transformation: Write a letter to yourself, acknowledging the existence of your bad habits without judgment. Express acceptance of these habits as part of

your journey. Explore how embracing them might lead to transformation and growth.

Questions to Ponder:

1. Observation and Awareness: How closely do you observe your bad habits? Are you aware of the circumstances and emotions surrounding these habits? Reflect on the level of attention you give to your own behaviors.

2. Joy and Craving: Consider a specific bad habit. Reflect on the joy or satisfaction you derive from it. Can you identify an underlying craving that this habit satisfies? How does understanding this craving impact your perspective on the habit?

3. Guilt and Society's Influence: Explore the role of guilt in your life. How much of it is influenced by societal norms and external expectations? In what ways can you challenge and reprogram your mindset to reduce the impact of guilt?

4. Acceptance and Transformation: How comfortable are you with accepting your bad habits without judgment? Reflect on the concept that acceptance might lead to transformation. Are you open to the idea of your relationship with these habits evolving naturally?

5. Door Holding Analogy: Consider the analogy of holding the door against a bad habit. How often do you find yourself resisting, and what energy does it consume? Explore the idea of allowing the habit in, understanding it, and befriending it. What changes could this perspective bring to your relationship with the habit?

9.
BATTLE PLAN FROM THE MOUNTAIN TOP

A lesson from history. Don't worry... No dates to memorize here. Let's talk about Game of Thrones and the battles portrayed. A good battle plan is made from the height of the mountain top. Even the miniature plans are for the same purpose. Better perspective. Each day is not exactly a battle, but then it still kinda is. In its own way.

Once the battle begins on the ground, the strategy which is already thought out is put in action. Trying to make strategy while on the ground and the battle is going on is a sure recipe for defeat. Yes, improvisation is a good thing. But the core structure still remains based on a strategy made before entering the battle.

The same applies to the day plan. Here too, the strategy includes the main plan, backup plan, and tactics for escape if you get stuck in any unplanned situation. It also includes entertainment and pleasure parts so that while in battle, the mind doesn't start day-dreaming. ;-)

The shortest plan can be for the next 24 hours. This is a practical and foreseeable timeline. Even this is unpredictable because we generally can't predict how the mood will be at the end of the day. But for practical purposes, it is a good span to begin planning.

"If you can see only up to the next few steps and still you decide to keep walking with awareness, it will take you far."

The key is to plan before the day begins. Plan with priorities to the pleasurable part. Inner needs are very important. If you create space in your schedule, distractions will decrease.

It is almost like, taking care of the most notorious kid in the group first. The rest will be easy to manage after that.

Exercises:

1. Mountain-Top Visualization: Find a quiet space and visualize yourself standing on a mountain top, overseeing the landscape of your life. Imagine crafting a battle plan for your upcoming day from this vantage point. What elements would you include in your plan, and how does this perspective influence your decisions?

2. Daily Battle Plan Journal: Create a daily battle plan journal. In the morning, before starting your day, jot down your main plan, backup plan, and potential tactics for handling unexpected situations. Reflect on the pleasure

and entertainment elements you've included. In the evening, revisit your journal to see how your actual day aligned with your planned strategy.

Questions to Ponder:

1. Battlefield Perspective: How often do you approach your daily challenges from a "mountain-top" perspective, gaining a broader view before diving into the details? How might this perspective shift influence your decision-making and overall mindset?

2. Inner Needs and Distractions: Reflect on the importance of prioritizing inner needs and incorporating pleasurable activities into your daily battle plan. How do these elements contribute to a more focused and undivided mindset, and how can you ensure they receive adequate attention in your planning?

3. Adaptability vs. Core Structure: Consider the balance between adaptability and core structure in your daily plans. How open are you to improvisation during the day, and to what extent do you rely on the core structure you've established beforehand?

10.
A SYSTEM WITHOUT LEAKAGE

A ship has a water-tight design. There cannot be any leakage. We, too, perform better in our lives in the same way. By protecting the time + energy + attention from any leakage. You can create wonder by putting these resources to use without waste.

One miraculous outcome of this exercise is the creation of time. Yes, time is a finite resource, and we have no control over it. I agree. But when you seal the leakage, the time which was going down the drain is now available for proper use.

Imagine you have designed proper time slots for pleasurable activities. Your mind now knows that you have made a contract with yourself to fulfill this commitment. There will be no distraction while you focus on deep work in the present moment. This kind of deep work brings many more creative ideas. Your focused attention on a subject (one at a time) is like nourishment to the brain. It brings many more creative ideas.

"Commit yourself to proper time slots for pleasure activities. Follow it up as planned. This clears the mind space for focused work which will be distraction-free!"

This simple arrangement with the self is enough. You would not need much greater willpower to assert your willpower to stick to the tasks. Now this precious willpower is available for all your important assignments. And this is how it should be. Will power to keep away from checking media is a very poor use of such a valuable resource.

A point will come when a realization hits you. The loss of resources to date has been big. This is a sign that you are ready to continue working on repairs. You'd wonder why you got so late thinking like this for such an important thing.

Exercises:

1. Time Audit: Take some time to audit how you currently allocate your time, energy, and attention throughout the day. Identify areas where there may be leaks or inefficiencies in your system. Then, brainstorm practical solutions to seal these leaks and optimize your resource allocation.

2. Leakage Prevention Plan: Create a leakage prevention plan for yourself, focusing on strategies to protect your time, energy, and attention from unnecessary drains. This could include setting boundaries with technology, scheduling regular breaks to recharge, and prioritizing tasks based on their importance and impact.

Questions to Ponder:

1. Resource Allocation Reflection: Reflect on how effectively you currently allocate your time, energy, and attention. Are there areas where you notice significant leaks or inefficiencies? What steps can you take to improve your resource allocation and prevent further leakage?

2. Impact of Sealed Leaks: Imagine a scenario where you successfully seal all the leaks in your time, energy, and attention. How do you think this would impact your productivity, creativity, and overall well-being? What benefits do you anticipate from having a more streamlined and efficient system?

3. Value of Willpower: Consider the role of willpower in maintaining an undivided focus and preventing leakage in your system. How can you conserve and prioritize your willpower for tasks that truly matter, rather than expending it on resisting distractions or temptations?

11.
CODE YOUR BRAIN

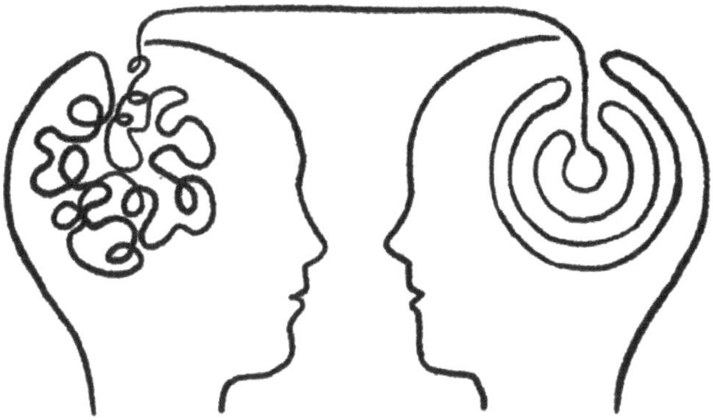

This may sound too complex, but actually is simple. The problem is, we start from the wrong direction. Wait. Let me explain before you get funny ideas.

You must prioritize the not-so-essential activities (from the point of view of others, not yours!). Otherwise, those random pop-ups from those activities will keep distracting you. Sound counterintuitive? That's because no other "expert" told you so ever before!

You may still get phases of daydreams about pleasurable activities. This is normal. And in time it will autocorrect. Because your mind will be getting self-reminders about the allotted time slot. And you can continue with the current task and stay in the deep work zone. I am eager to share in the following section how you can program your 24-hour cycle.
A rule of coding is to compartmentalize the module for cleanliness and easy edits. This applies to brain coding as well. When the major items are clear and well separated, the flow is beautiful.

"The first place to use all your creativity is while coding your brain. Own your self and the rest is just details."

Giving priority to pleasure activities has one distinct benefit. You stay distraction free even in these wonderful activities. Distractions from the saintly personality are on mute. This creates the right climate for a deep and guilt-free focus on the pleasure part.

You will find a lot of room for improvement and modification. The fruitful outcome of clarity and peace will lead your way.

Remember not to overload the system with too many expectations. There are age-old programs still residing in the system. There will be resistance from inside. Why? Because you may go unconscious many times, and the old programs flex their muscles. Every player experiences this. It is ok. Softly get back to the planned game. Simple!

We will have all the necessary checks and balances for such times when the going gets tough. It will be a continuous upgrade of the system which learns from every step and keep getting evolved. Over a short period, the exponential factor will start to kick in. If I can predict the future, I'd say you too would want to write your own book about this magical phenomenon!

Exercises:

1. Brain Coding Activity: Take some time to map out your daily activities and prioritize them based on their importance and impact on your overall well-being. Use a simple chart or diagram to visualize this coding of your brain. Identify areas where you can compartmentalize tasks for better organization and focus.

2. Pleasure Activity Schedule: Create a schedule or timetable specifically allocating time slots for pleasurable activities that you enjoy. This could include hobbies, relaxation, or socializing with friends and family. Stick to this schedule for a week and observe how it affects your overall productivity and mindset.

Questions to Ponder:

1. Prioritizing Pleasure: Reflect on the concept of prioritizing pleasure activities in your daily schedule. How does this approach differ from conventional productivity advice? What benefits do you anticipate from giving importance to activities that bring you joy and fulfillment, even if they may seem non-essential to others?

2. Resistance and Adaptation: Consider the idea that resistance from old programming may arise when trying to implement new habits and routines. How do you plan to navigate this resistance and stay committed to your brain coding efforts? What strategies can you employ to adapt and evolve your system over time, despite encountering challenges?

12.
“IN-DIVIDUAL”, SERIOUSLY?

You think you are an individual. Now, if you pay attention to this word. It is made of two parts, “in” and “dividual”. It means you are non-dividable. Ok, accepted that you can’t have your arm to go out independently and work for you. Or your eyes fly out high and get an aerial shot. Um.. at least not in the current times. Maybe in the far away future.

What I am pointing towards is deep inside you. For example, when you wake up in the morning (if you do.. Some are afternoon people!) you don’t have any clue about your probable mood by the time you go back to sleep at night. We all carry a large bunch of different versions within us like A, B, C... to Z, and some more. And each one is in conflict with the others. They keep fighting for the captain position in the game. After one gets to the leadership position, it will condemn the previous captain. This may bring up the feeling of guilt.

As a matter of fact, all these splits are the result of modern world design. The impression you intake results in chemical variation in the body-brain. Society at large gives us a false/rigid/myopic understanding of the good/bad model. And a funny thing about the good/bad model is, it changes constantly over a period of time as society goes through cyclic changes.

“All the splits within you are uniquely wonderful players. Build a united team that works as an individual and reinvent the game!”

Whatever you have and what you will eventually own will be multiplied by who you are from inside. My theory is, if you are divided, you are less than one. You are just the fraction of

1 divided by the number of splits you carry within you. The lesser splits you have, the better quality of the number you are. From say 0.1 to 0.2 to 0.5 to finally reach the end of the process when no splits remain, and you become one! Sounds like Morpheus with a mysterious smile professing to Neo from the movie "Matrix", isn't it?

Everything else that you earn outside adds up like zeros to the one yourself. And the growth compounds exponentially. Now, probably the title of the book should start to make more sense. It is pointless to go out in search of treasure when you don't have earned your very own self. So starting with self-unification must be the natural first step.

Exercises:

1. Inner Dialogue Journal: Throughout the day, observe the different "versions" or aspects of yourself that emerge in different situations or moods. Keep a journal and note down these observations, including any conflicting thoughts or emotions you experience. Reflect on what triggers these different versions and how they interact with each other.

2. Self-Integration Visualization: Set aside some quiet time for meditation or visualization. Close your eyes and imagine all the different aspects of yourself coming together as one cohesive entity. Visualize each part contributing its strengths and qualities to create a unified and empowered version of yourself. Pay attention to any resistance or acceptance you feel during this exercise.

Questions to Ponder:

1. Understanding Inner Splits: Reflect on the concept of inner splits or conflicting aspects within yourself. How do these different versions of yourself manifest in your daily life? Are there specific situations or triggers that tend to bring out certain aspects more than others? How do these splits impact your overall well-being and decision-making process?

2. The Journey to Self-Unification: Consider the idea that achieving self-unification is a process of becoming whole and integrated. How do you envision your journey towards uniting the different parts of yourself? What steps can you take to embrace and integrate the various aspects of your personality and inner world? How might this process contribute to your overall growth and self-improvement?

13.
THINK FROM THE RIGHT PLACE!

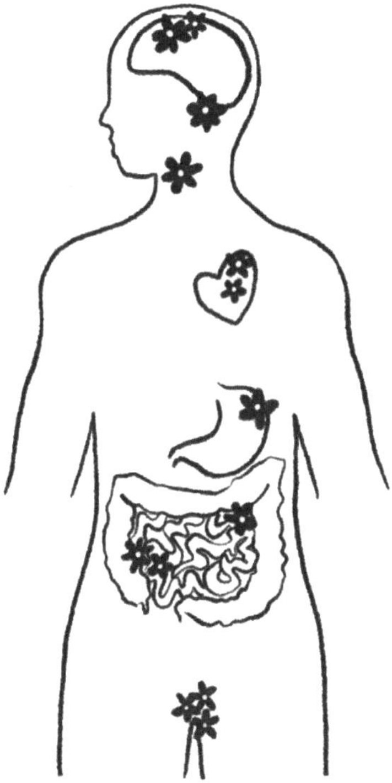

So you think, you use your head for all your decisions. Hmm.. Let me pin the balloon by saying that you have been kidding yourself. There are at least 4 other organs in your body that affect how your head works. Funny thing, but true. Let me prove it.

Now the first point applied only to mature adults but even for growing teenage, this will be vital for the future. This organ is the genitalia. Once the hormonal gland starts to work, it affects all decisions. Most of the time, sheer intensity of this organ deactivates the head even in big decisions of life. To find a mate, life partner, business partner, and any companion selection process. It is a vital input to the head while making decisions, and I would like to warn you here. This part of your body is not a reliable decision-maker itself. Hope you get my point.

The next up is your guts. We hear people talking confidently about gut feelings. It is a vital part of decision-making, but it is not the complete picture. It is just an accumulation of experiences of self or others learned through stories of people. Nature has given all animals this sense of protection and such. It is a vital input to the head for decision-making.

"Avoid big decisions when hungry. Focus on deciding the menu first!"

Further upwards is the stomach. Just like a popular TV ad. I think it was some chocolate bar. It was hilarious. A perfect depiction of how people turn into a monster when hungry. And return to normal when they eat the chocolate bar.

The next big one is the heart. La..La..La.. Yeah, the singing dancing crying heart. A lot of colors here, but these colors may cloud the judgments. It is an essential part of life, and still not the complete decision-making element. Give it enough space, understand its waves and whims, and flow with it sometimes. But be careful not to flow away with it.

Finally, we come to head. The central command works well only when the other four are working under its leadership. The lower four are in line and ready to give and take inputs fo better decision-making. The head must remain "the head" of the whole system. The Head must remain open to listen to the other four parts with complete attention. The head decides the course of action based on proper evaluation of the inputs from the lower four. This is a sure recipe for a good life.

I call the inputs from the lower four points a cocktail of emotions. The head has to check the situation without too much emotional angle for better clarity. By giving appropriate weightage to each input. And arriving at a decision that stands the test of time is a good strategy.

Exercises:

1. Body Scan Meditation: Set aside some quiet time for a body scan meditation. Sit or lie down comfortably and close your eyes. Start by focusing on your breath, then gradually shift your attention to different parts of your body, starting from your feet and moving up to your head. Notice any sensations, tensions, or emotions that arise in each area. Reflect on how these physical sensations and emotions may influence your decision-making process.

2. Emotional Mapping Exercise: Take a piece of paper and draw a simple outline of a body. Label each major organ (genitalia, guts, stomach, heart, head) and jot down any emotions or feelings associated with each one. Reflect on how these emotions impact your decision-making in different situations. Consider how you can maintain balance and clarity by integrating inputs from each part.

Questions to Ponder:

1. Understanding the Influence of Different Organs: Reflect on the concept that decision-making involves inputs from various organs beyond just the head. How aware are you of the influence that your genitalia, guts, stomach, heart, and head have on your decision-making process? Can you

recall instances where decisions were influenced by factors other than logical reasoning or rational thought?

2. Balancing Emotions and Rationality: Consider the balance between emotional responses and rational thinking in decision-making. How do you navigate situations where your emotions may cloud your judgment? Are there strategies you can employ to ensure that decisions are made with clarity and balance, taking into account inputs from both your emotions and your logical reasoning?

GET READY FOR HOW

14.
WATCH THE GAME WITHOUT SCORECARD

Ever played a game without a scorecard? It is super fun. And why shouldn't it be? All free hit. There's no performance pressure. And no rules. I wish life would have been like that!

Anyway, this is a method to revive memory of many things you do but don't remember that you do. Yes, your memory is highly selective. And it deletes everything which is either unimportant or not very enjoyable for you.

There are layers. From big events that affect people around you to micro gestures and bodily movements that happens as signals from deep subconscious. Sometimes people around you would notice them. And they would create an image of you in their minds. It may happen that you disagree completely with them when they share with you.

This reminds of a few of our dear friends. When they are drunk, we see a whole new person in them. We take it as a usual thing. But look deeper. There is a split inside them. The front facade falls off with liquor. And the part which was held back for a long time becomes free to express all the suppressed emotions. I see this as a therapy. Hey, that doesn't mean you can begin drinking.

Just give them this book. They need to become "Undivided". And let there be no separate parts. There is no need for suppressing.

A game without scorecard makes you see yourself without masks and makeup.

And the first step in self therapy is to watch your game without a scorecard. Observe your own behavior. Physical and mental. Keep a nice journal. A therapy begins with diagnosis. You got to know the current situation to make necessary treatment.

This is like finding out opening balance in your books of account before opening for business. Your point A. The starting point. This will give you a clear reference point. The process of transformation can now begin.

Exercises:

1. Mirror Reflection Exercise: Spend a few minutes each day looking at yourself in the mirror without any judgment or preconceived notions. Simply observe your facial expressions, body language, and gestures. Notice any subtle changes or reactions that occur as you observe yourself. Reflect on what these observations reveal about your inner state and emotions.

2. Day in Review Journal: At the end of each day, take some time to reflect on your experiences and actions. Write down key events, interactions, and emotions that occurred throughout the day. Be honest and objective in your reflections, without censoring or sugar-coating anything. Reviewing your journal entries over time can help you gain insight into patterns of behavior and areas for personal growth.

Questions to Ponder:

1. Self-Reflection and Awareness: How often do you take the time to observe and reflect on your own thoughts, emotions, and behaviors without judgment? What are some barriers that prevent you from engaging in self-reflection, and how can you overcome them? Reflect on the importance of developing self-awareness as a foundation for personal growth and self-improvement.

2. Unmasking the True Self: Consider the concept of "watching the game without a scorecard" as a means of unmasking your true self. How does the absence of judgment and external validation influence your perception of yourself? Reflect on any insights or revelations that arise from observing yourself without the need to conform to societal expectations or personal biases.

15.
A CLOSED-DOOR MEETING WITH SELF

This is the most important thing you need to do asap. You have been fumbling with things and people and ideas, but it only increased chaos.

Chill and escape to solitude for a short break. Be alone. You can go for a walk without gadgets. You can sit in the bathroom. Find a place. Come back to your breath. Exhale and confirm that you are alive and in your own body.

Now, look at your mind. Many things float at a fast speed. It is usually like a dust storm. Nothing clearly visible. Numerous thoughts and the speed of those thoughts. Almost like dust particles flying furiously. All you can do here is watch and not get in this storm. You can not stop it. All your efforts to stop it will only increase the speed. Sit easy and watch as if watching the storm through a glass window of your palace.

This is an opportunity to see many minds inside your mind. Yes, each is like a separate program with its own agenda. And each one has a strong opinion against the other programs. Think of them as players of a team who are not on good talking terms with one another. As if the team is designed to lose. And each player blames all the other players.

"When a team is divided, the result is obvious. A united team is open to possibilities and stands together in every situation."

What is that you want to do wholeheartedly? Ok. In simple word, is there anything on which you are not divided? A part of you want to do something but another part of you is opposing that.

The meeting is to focus on making these two opposing parts come to common ground. Yes, usually you let the jump happen. Once you gain consciousness, the opposing part makes you feel so much guilty. We can not let this go on.

Remember those sports movies? A wise and experienced coach who brings the team together. Each player has to respect all the other players. No matter who is the captain, all players support the decisions. And each decision taken includes all players. The team starts to perform slightly better. The bonding between players improves step by step.

This takes the team to a new high and happiness. A united team is like the greatest gift to the members of the team. A closed-door meeting with the self is for understanding each player. This will resolve the differences between team members. Do it every day religiously. Yes, this may sound like a cheesy prescription. Write back to me your experiences on this point.

Exercises:

1. Mindful Breathing Meditation: Find a quiet and comfortable space where you can sit or lie down without distractions. Close your eyes and bring your attention to your breath. Notice the sensation of each inhale and exhale. As thoughts arise, simply observe them without judgment and gently bring your focus back to your breath. Practice this for 5-10 minutes daily to cultivate mindfulness and calmness.

2. Inner Dialogue Journaling: Set aside time each day to engage in inner dialogue journaling. Write down any conflicting thoughts, emotions, or desires that arise within you. Explore each perspective with curiosity and compassion, allowing each "player" in your mind to express itself fully. Reflect on the underlying motivations and beliefs behind these conflicting parts of yourself.

Questions to Ponder:

1. Integration of Opposing Parts: Reflect on the different aspects of yourself that seem to be in conflict or opposition. What are some common themes or patterns among these opposing parts? How can you work towards integrating these parts and finding common ground within yourself? Consider the potential benefits of inner unity and alignment in achieving your goals and fostering personal growth.
2. Team Dynamics Within Yourself: Imagine your inner dialogue as a team of players with different roles and agendas. How do these "players" interact with each other? Are there certain players that dominate the conversation, while others are sidelined or ignored? Reflect on the dynamics within your internal team and consider strategies for fostering collaboration and harmony among its members.

16.
CONTRACT WITH SELF

Let's begin. I suggest to use paper/diary 📓 and pen/pencil. ✏️ The brain works better when you scribble on paper. The safest technique to preserve your ideas and plans. And yes, I will eventually include the use of electronics, so have patience!

I am going into all details, so you have no major questions left, and the process begins with a head start.

1. Write the day and date on the top.

2. Split the page in half. Fold the page for reference, or draw a line in the middle.

3. On the left side. Begin writing.

4. List down morning wake-up time to sleep time.

5. The big and unchangeable items of your routine are clear to you. Write it down.

6. Now the most important part. The pleasurable activities. You know what attracts your mind constantly. Pick the best time for it and give it sufficient slot size.

7. Now let's welcome and include the bad habits. Give it a suitable time slot in the day. Or check boxes for the number of times you plan to do it.

8. The remaining time, if there is any, mark it with a tag, free. Think of all you wanted to learn/read/watch. Utilize it to upgrade yourself with useful knowledge.

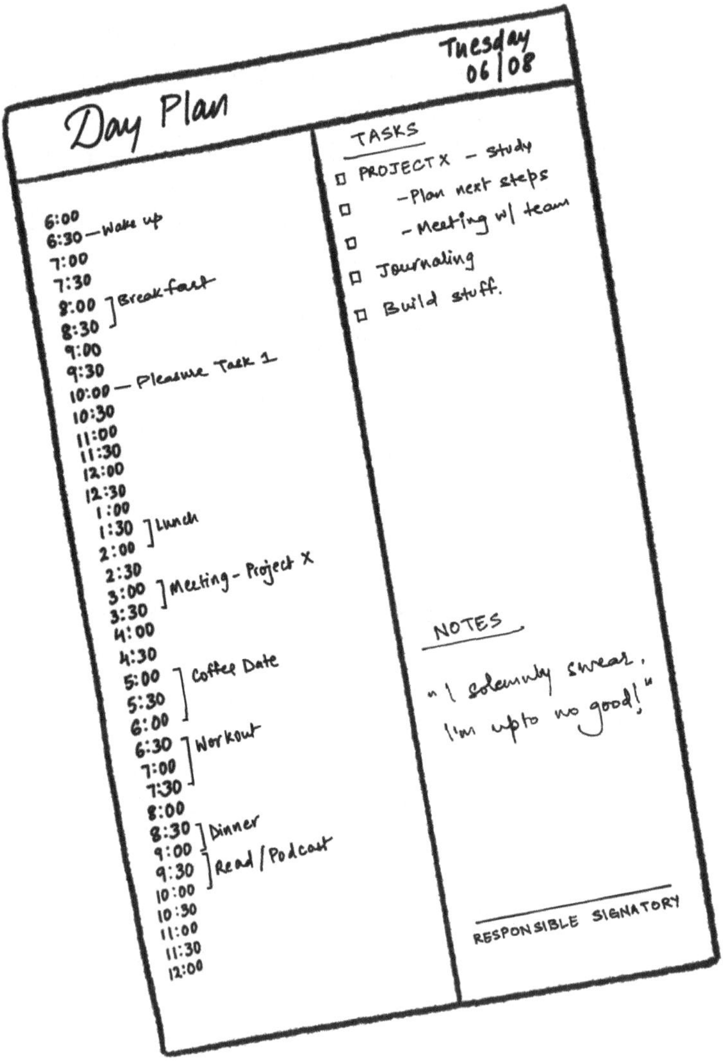
Day Plan
Tuesday 06/08
6:00
6:30 — Wake up
7:00
7:30
8:00
8:30 Breakfast
9:00
9:30
10:00 — Pleasure Task 1
10:30
11:00
11:30
12:00
12:30
1:00
1:30 Lunch
2:00
2:30
3:00
3:30 Meeting - Project X
4:00
4:30
5:00
5:30
6:00 Coffee Date
6:30
7:00
7:30 Workout
8:00
8:30 Dinner
9:00
9:30 Read / Podcast
10:00
10:30
11:00
11:30
12:00
TASKS
PROJECT X — Study
— Plan next steps
— Meeting w/ team
Journaling
Build stuff.
NOTES
"I solemnly swear, I'm upto no good!"
RESPONSIBLE SIGNATORY

9. As an option, allow yourself to waste the free slot or take rest. Sip tea/coffee.

"Your brain needs a plan. Better make it yourself or else everyone around will make and force it upon you!"

10. Be specific about checking your phone. My suggestion is to allow yourself to check the phone for random media checking only at every O' Clock only. For up to 5 minutes.

11. All the routine quirks are included in the day plan contract and if there is any missing, it will show up as you start the day. Note down such deviations and include them when you draw the next day's plan.

12. Sign at the bottom of the page. Yes, it is mandatory. You're making a conscious commitment to yourself. You have to sign. And stand by your signature.

Right Column

Everything else that falls spontaneously during the day goes into the right side column. There are a few ways to tackle it. One is to return to them in free slots and include them in the next day's plan. You have to use your best judgment for this. Just one caution. Do not let your reflex possess you to jump into this spontaneous task. Write it down first. More about the right column coming up ahead.

Exercises:

1. Daily Planning Exercise: Use the described method to create a detailed daily plan for tomorrow. Follow each step carefully, noting down your wake-up and sleep times, allocating slots for pleasurable activities, bad habits, learning opportunities, and free time. Sign the contract at the bottom of the page as a commitment to yourself.

2. Reflection and Adjustment: At the end of the day, review your daily plan and the events that unfolded. Reflect on how closely you followed your plan and whether any unexpected tasks or distractions arose. Consider what adjustments you could make to improve your planning process and better align with your goals and priorities.

Questions to Ponder:

1. Commitment to Self: How does signing the contract at the bottom of the page impact your sense of accountability and commitment to yourself? Reflect on the significance of making conscious commitments to prioritize your well-being and personal growth.

2. Balancing Structure and Flexibility: How do you strike a balance between following a structured daily plan and allowing flexibility for spontaneous tasks or distractions? Consider the importance of adaptability in maintaining your commitment to self-growth while also being responsive to unexpected events or opportunities.

17.

VISUALIZE THE EVENTS 👀

I am sure you have watched espionage movies. The ones in which the lead character is in the Secret Service. And the lead character is sent on a mission. Remember how this mission is visualized before it is undertaken. The flow of events to happen one after another, and the backup plans if things go south.

This is a powerful technique in many professions. In sports, athletes and players visualize the event with their planned strategy in mind. In dramas, movie making, and dance performances this method is an intrinsic part.

The same technique is useful for us to design a wonderful day. It is easy as you start practicing and doesn't take much time if you are a busy professional.

Let me help you jumpstart the visualization. Begin at the time when you wake up and open your eyes. Flow through the usual routine. You may come across things that you want to change. For example, the first thing you do could be to pick up the phone. But you always think it is not a good idea, change that in your visualization. Keep moving through your day as you have planned on paper.

"The amount of energy saved by planning and visualizing a single day is magical. You will create productive time worth many days!"

Add all the details as you become proficient in this practice of visualization. Small details like pausing at every door before crossing. It is a good strategy to remind yourself that everything you need is with you. Keys, wallet, purse, phone, headphones.. the little stuff that often get misplaced and takes a lot of time and energy to get back.

There is so much energy going to waste in our routine because we stop to decide small things every step of the way. From deciding about clothes in the morning to what to eat for breakfast and so on. These may seem small things to plan. But such advance planning has a huge outcome. There will be a lot of energy and time available when you truly need your ability to think and decide important things.

You will be amazed at the possibilities that open up when you clean up the mess. It will be like a powerful takeoff from the runway of entanglements. There is a lot of learning on this planet and you will see it clearly once the mundane is overcome by taking care of it consciously.

Exercises:

1. Day Visualization Practice: Set aside 5-10 minutes each morning to visualize your day ahead. Close your eyes and imagine yourself moving through your day from the moment you wake up until you go to bed. Picture yourself completing tasks, engaging in pleasurable activities, and handling any challenges that may arise. Try to visualize with as much detail as possible, including your surroundings, actions, and emotions.

2. Visualization Journaling: After completing your day visualization, jot down key points or insights that came to you during the exercise. Reflect on any adjustments or improvements you want to make to your daily routine based on what you visualized. Use this journaling practice

to track your progress and refine your visualization skills over time.

Questions to Ponder:

1. Impact of Visualization: How does visualizing your day in advance affect your mindset and approach to daily tasks? Reflect on any shifts in motivation, focus, or productivity that you experience as a result of incorporating visualization into your routine.

2. Alignment with Goals: Are there any discrepancies between your visualized day and your long-term goals or aspirations? Consider how aligning your daily actions with your overarching goals can help you cultivate a sense of purpose and direction in your life.

18.
AUTOMATE THE ESSENTIALS

I have been an average person about planning my schedules, but a few things I can vouch for that works on their own after I made them automatic in my routine. Yes, the single most powerful trick was to earn joy out of the activity. If it is dry and chore-like, the brain will eventually push it aside and also find reasons to do so.

Morning workout (sounds bitter? Wait.. I'm about to make it sweeter!) has been one such automatic activity. I have designed my own Warm-up stretches > 21 sets mix of upper body + core + Lower body movements of HIIT > Cooldown stretches. This is what I do in the morning the second thing after that mandatory detox.

I have realized that this is automatic because the brain loves this activation system of full-body charging. It is intended less for physical and more for brain activation, and believe me, it bloody works. And the mood gets better and hunger to take a good breakfast too. Maybe that's why I don't have to plan for it or use any willpower at all.

And this made me see that when I automate my routine activities and add an element of fun to them, the brain just makes it happen without my interference.

You need to be creative to make any activity fun and set a time slot for it. The rest will happen automatically.

"Willpower is a precious resource. Utilize it sparingly for special tasks. Automate the routine."

And this automation will slowly build up over a period of time, be it physical work, mental work, or daily chores. The inner chemistry will build up to facilitate you going into the mood without friction, and the energy can be put to productive use right away.

Exercises:

1. Create a Joyful Morning Routine: Take some time to brainstorm and design a morning routine that includes activities you genuinely enjoy. This could involve a mix of physical exercises, mindfulness practices, creative hobbies, or anything else that energizes you. Experiment with different combinations until you find a routine that feels uplifting and invigorating.

2. Implement Habit Stacking: Identify an existing habit in your daily routine, such as brushing your teeth or making coffee, and stack a new activity onto it. For example, if you want to incorporate reading into your day, you could commit to reading for 10 minutes while waiting for your coffee to brew. By linking new habits to existing ones, you can make them more automatic and effortless over time.

Questions to Ponder:

1. What Activities Bring You Joy?
   Reflect on the activities or tasks that naturally uplift your mood and bring you a sense of fulfillment. How can you incorporate more of these joyful activities into your daily routine to automate and streamline your schedule?

2. How Can You Infuse Fun into Routine Tasks?
   Consider how you can add an element of fun or creativity to mundane tasks or responsibilities. Whether it's listening to music while doing chores, turning workouts into a game, or finding humor in everyday activities, brainstorm ways to make routine tasks more enjoyable and engaging.

19.
CONTRACT BREAKERS

This may happen. And it is very important what I am going to say now. Incidents of breaking the contract will happen in the beginning. Now, look at the good part. You are able to see the breaking point because you made a contract with yourself. It is like, if you made a dam and the channels are not well-developed, the water would spill out.

All you have to do here is to note down the points where you broke the contract. And in the next contract, thoughtfully include those points and events. Give appropriate time and space, and be inclusive and warm-hearted.

It is a reminder from the subconscious mind. And acceptance is the way to go forwards without any friction. This constant observation of your daily events, noting down what comes up, and upgrading the routine is a continuous process. It helps keep the mind running like a fine-tuned engine or, in a modern context, an auto bug-fixing system.

Point is, don't give up the process just because you might find many cracks. It is part of the process. And cracks are initial bugs in the code. It is completely natural and, in fact, extremely helpful. Just make sure they are meticulously taken note of. And begin including them.

"The first draft will obviously have bugs. Keep upgrading the Versions to fix these bugs!"

This is like creating new canals. It is based on daily observation about where the resources are better needed. And at the same time, you will be able to manage the dam based on how much you have in stock and how much to spend.

Right column

Suddenly, you will be reminded of something you wanted to browse on the net. Or the phone call you should make. Or saying a silly hello to the old flame you always wanted to get closer to. It's ok. Yeah, seriously! But, don't jump on the phone. Just write it down in the blank right column. We left it just for this purpose. Our free slots are just right for these minis. And if it's a bigger task than the free slot size, there's an even better solution.

Then you begin to write a plan for the next day, including all these floating tasks and thoughts in the new plan.

In simple words, the plans you made will show cracks in the initial trials. Keep sealing these cracks with necessary modifications and keep moving forward.

Exercises:

1. Contract Breakdown Analysis: Take some time to review instances where you broke your self-contract or deviated from your planned routine. Write down the specific circumstances or triggers that led to these breaks. Reflect on whether these breaks were due to external factors, internal resistance, or unforeseen challenges. Use this information to develop strategies for overcoming similar obstacles in the future.

2. Adapt and Upgrade Your Contract: Based on the insights gained from analyzing contract breaches, revise and upgrade your daily contract with yourself. Identify areas where adjustments are needed to better align with your

goals and values. Consider adding contingency plans or alternative approaches to address potential challenges proactively.

Questions to Ponder:

1. What Patterns Do You Notice in Your Contract Breaks?
   Reflect on recurring themes or patterns in the instances where you've deviated from your planned routine. Are there specific times of day, environmental cues, or emotional states that seem to trigger these breaks? How can you address these patterns to minimize future disruptions?

2. How Can You Respond to Contract Breaks with Compassion and Understanding?
   Consider how you typically react when you break your self-contract. Are you self-critical or compassionate towards yourself? How might you cultivate a mindset of self-compassion and acceptance when facing setbacks or deviations from your plan?

20.
KEEP YOUR PROMISES

The promises that you give to yourself are the most important ones. Okay. Second most important ones.
I know, right?

I can assure you this works like magic. Under the contract with self, we talked about giving schedules and time slots to pleasurable activities. One funny thing which may happen when you start rolling with this system is. And that is an expansion of the ego. You start to feel that you're very powerful, and you don't have to keep all the promises you give yourself. And let me tell you, that may bring a halt to the game.

The part of your mind may start to lose trust in the other part. The dominating part likes to play the boss. Giving time slot to pleasurable activities may make that part of the mind quiet till the time arrive. And just because it waited patiently, you think you can ignore it and skip the pleasurable slot completely. You are mistaken. This is a breach of the contract. This may jeopardize the beginning of a friendship between parts of your mind.

It is possible, going forward, that part of the mind might plot an even twisted storyline. It just may get difficult to get back on track. This is like playing hide and seek with self. Not a great strategy. A lot of energy might be lost.

And for genuine reasons, you find yourself unable to fulfill the promise, explain in detail to that part of your mind. In detail. Stand in front of the mirror. The mind will understand. There will be no baggage. The game of life will improve.

Exercises:

1. Reflective Journaling: Set aside time each day to reflect on whether you kept the promises you made to yourself. Write down any instances where you upheld your commitments and moments where you fell short. Explore the reasons behind any breaches of your self-contract and consider how you can address them moving forward.

2. Visualization and Affirmations: Spend a few minutes each morning visualizing yourself successfully keeping the promises you've made to yourself throughout the day. Use affirmations such as "I honor my commitments to myself" or "I am reliable and trustworthy to myself" to reinforce your dedication to following through on your self-promises.

Questions to Ponder:

1. What Internal Dialogue Do You Have When Tempted to Break a Promise to Yourself?
2. Reflect on the thoughts and feelings that arise when you're tempted to skip a commitment you've made to yourself. Are there recurring patterns in your internal dialogue? How can you shift your mindset to prioritize honoring your promises to yourself?
3. How Can You Cultivate a Sense of Accountability to Yourself?

4. Consider strategies for holding yourself accountable to the promises you make. Are there external reminders or support systems you can put in place to help you stay on track? How can you foster a sense of self-trust and reliability in your relationship with yourself?

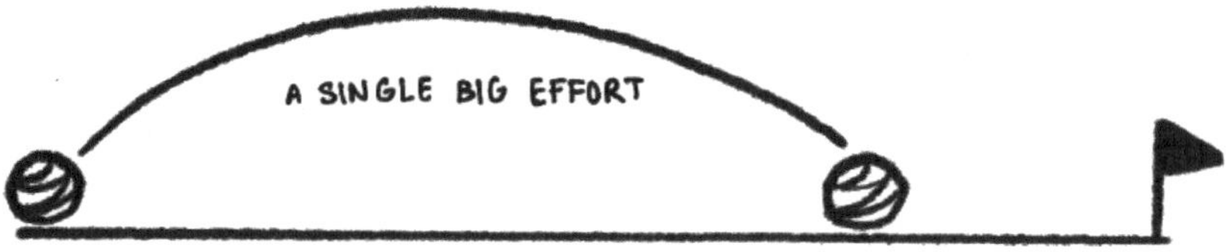
A SINGLE BIG EFFORT

SMALL SNEAKY STEPS OVER TIME

21.
FALL SEVEN TIMES...

stand up eight times. The resistance from the inner system will show up when you try to take control in your hands. Few obvious things will happen.

For example, You will not feel like writing the day plan. Your mind will say it is pointless and not going to work. You may find it difficult to remember the timing of tasks, and thus the schedule will not be met. Use the reminders app on your phone.

You may misplace the journal/diary/paper where the plan is written. (Your subconscious mind will play tricks!)

One small whim to do something out of the planned flow and the rest of the plan will fall apart.

Fear of failure will keep you away from such a noble challenge to take control of life.

You are much habituated to a messed up work-life flow. In the beginning, the new structure will feel too good to be true and kinda alien!

Slavery is a safe environment for many. Slavery to the outer environment. It will need a strong resolve to break this.

"The old habit of unconscious living is easy to break with small and sneaky steps!"

It is always ok to restart from the fresh. Painters and writers and artists of all sorts experience this. The first attempt is a stepping stone to the next attempt. Learn to be an artist who is waking up to redesign life. It is a long and beautiful journey where every step is reaching higher than the previous one. Sometimes, one may stumble and fall. Make a good note of this and get back to revise and strengthen the future plans.

To convert a difficult task into an easy one, there is one time-tested method. Do a little bit every day. Eventually, it will become kind of second nature. After a short while, you will not have to give a lot of energy to it, and you will start to feel as if it is happening on its own!

Your subconscious remembers the joy you had while experimenting with a new way of living. The old habits may pull you down sometimes. Accept it as a part of the process. The memories of flying will give you the courage and strength to stand up and attempt to fly again. A time will come when the falls will only be the trips downward to learn something useful.

Exercises:

1. Daily Reflection: At the end of each day, take a few minutes to reflect on any challenges you faced in sticking to your plans or commitments. Write down what caused these setbacks and brainstorm potential solutions or adjustments you can make to prevent similar obstacles in the future.

2. Progress Journal: Keep a journal dedicated to documenting your journey of self-growth and improvement. Record both your successes and setbacks, noting any patterns or recurring themes. Use this journal as a tool for self-reflection and as a source of motivation to keep pushing forward despite any obstacles.

Questions to Ponder:

1. How Can You Cultivate Resilience in the Face of Setbacks? Reflect on your past experiences of overcoming challenges or failures. What strategies or mindset shifts helped you bounce back from difficult situations? How can you apply these lessons to your current journey of self-growth and improvement?

2. What Role Does Self-Compassion Play in Your Journey of Self-Growth? Consider how you respond to yourself when you encounter setbacks or failures. Are you self-critical and harsh, or do you approach yourself with kindness and understanding? How can you cultivate a greater sense of self-compassion to support yourself through the ups and downs of your journey?

22.
USE YOUR IMAGINATION

There are more than enough things we are not able to do in life. The objects and people of desire are sometimes too far away from our reach.

Let's pause and think for once. Each one of us has a brain. (Presumably!) And this little machine has many extensions. They are in the form of a body with senses (eyes, ears, nose, tongue, skin). Each part of the body for it's a functional role to play in the game.

There is a constant flow of information going from these peripheral areas to the brain. The brain squeezes all this information to create a wholesome picture. A picture that makes more sense to make better decisions for a better life path forward. (See why most people seem to be unable to make better decisions? Their brains are somehow unable to do the most important task. And that is, creating an accurate picture!)

The point is, the brain creates pictures. And there are two ways to make pictures in the brain. One is the conventional way of relying on information inputs from peripheral organs. The other way is to imagine. And every living human is capable of a good imagination. Without even realizing, we are constantly imagining. It is just that we imagine the false worries and anxieties and the mess that we make, all in our heads.

“The whole world is like your imaginary single-player game!”

Now you remember you have the skill. Right? So let's learn to use that same skill in a different and useful way.

The thoughts floating in your head may be about objects of desire that are far away from you. Usually, we feel deprived of them and curse our destiny. This is not a healthy way.

For a moment, consider this idea. Be attentive to the floating thoughts that occupy your mind. Especially the thoughts which stay for longer periods with intensity. They make you lose track of time.

Take note of this and schedule a time for those thoughts.

Believe me, those thoughts will feel respected for getting the due attention. They may subside till the scheduled time to meet you again. I'd say these thoughts are living things. You need to learn to respect and communicate with them, you will earn new friends inside you.

Recurring thoughts are about incomplete desires. They are also about unprocessed incidents. They are about objects, activities, people, etc. All they need is your attention. Be attentive to them at a scheduled time to keep things compartmentalized and sane.

Something good emerges when these thoughts are resolved. The outcome is clarity and peace.

Exercises:

1. Imagination Journal: Set aside time each day to engage in imaginative exercises. Use your imagination to visualize your ideal life, career, relationships, or any other aspect you wish to improve. Write down your thoughts, feelings, and observations in a dedicated imagination journal. Use

this journal as a tool for exploring your desires and aspirations in a creative way.

2. Imaginary Exploration: Choose a specific goal or aspiration that feels out of reach or challenging to achieve. Close your eyes and imagine yourself successfully accomplishing this goal in vivid detail. Visualize the steps you took to get there, the obstacles you overcame, and the emotions you experienced along the way. Use this exercise to tap into your imagination's power to inspire and motivate you towards your goals.

Questions to Ponder:

1. How Can You Harness the Power of Your Imagination to Improve Your Life? Reflect on the ways in which you currently use your imagination in your daily life. How can you leverage your imaginative abilities to create positive change and pursue your goals with greater clarity and purpose?

2. What Role Does Visualization Play in Achieving Your Goals? Consider the connection between visualization and goal achievement. How does visualizing your desired outcomes impact your motivation, confidence, and sense of direction? How can you incorporate more visualization techniques into your routine to support your journey of self-growth and personal development?

23.
FIX THE STOMACH

First thing first. All that you are is not what you think. Yeah, Buddha said the opposite, but I changed it a little for you to make my point clear. I think, Buddha said a concise version, and it stands true for the eternity of mankind. Today's science confirms that good thinking stems from the quality of your stomach and, especially, the guts. I am saying stomach because it is about the complete digestive system.

It begins with your food choices. The next point is, how you chew the food. And also, what else you are doing while eating, how much water to gulp down before, during, and after the meal intake. The whole episode decides the efficiency of your digestion process. The end result is the quality of energy extracted from the food.

Next comes your food intake intervals/windows. The no-food time duration. Incognito, I'm hinting at intermittent fasting, and I can imagine my friends frowning!

Even if you have messed up your stomach by eating junk, there is simple therapy. Just give a small or medium, or large break to the stomach. It does wonders. It brings back the rhythm. Not only that, but it fixes the unbalanced elements to the recommended levels.

The point is to give good attention to what you are eating and when. This is an interesting topic and again a lot can be learned from the right sources and a few intelligent people. Those who have cracked the code of anti-aging and ultra wellness. They have brought back the ancient practice of fasting back into our time.

"Stomach is that secret kitchen for generating energy. It needs very good housekeeping and occasional holidays!"

The simple and everyday practicable method is an 8-hour eating window. In this window, feed yourself with a variety of eatables. And then for the remaining 16 hours, stop solid food intake. Anything above 14 hours of fasting is a good rest for the stomach. After that, the stomach gets rejuvenated to process the intake better.

I have realized that it keeps getting better as the stomach improves. This simple practice of giving long breaks to the stomach has a lot to offer for all kinds of personal growth.

There's one more thing. How you end the digestion process can not be ignored. Yes, the toilet. First thing first. Leave your phone outside the toilet. I don't know how you will do this challenging task, but I assure you it will be worth it. Or let it be in your pocket unless someone rings you for anything more urgent than excretion.

Your attention in this little game here can do wonders. Promise yourself to take good care of your body by being with it 100% while it is cleaning itself. This bond of friendship with your body will be the greatest long-term investment. A growth path to building a peaceful body and, of course, a clear mind.

Intermitent Fasting "clock"

Exercises:

1. Mindful Eating Practice: Set aside one mealtime each day to practice mindful eating. Sit down at a table without distractions such as phones or television. Take the time to chew your food slowly and savor each bite. Notice the flavors, textures, and sensations as you eat. Pay attention to how your body feels before, during, and after the meal. Reflect on the experience in a journal afterward.

2. Intermittent Fasting Experiment: Try incorporating intermittent fasting into your routine by limiting your eating window to 8 hours each day and fasting for the remaining 16 hours. Start with a small fasting window and gradually increase it as you become more comfortable. Pay attention to how your body responds to fasting, including changes in energy levels, digestion, and overall well-being.

Questions to Ponder:

1. How Does Your Diet Impact Your Overall Well-being? Reflect on your current eating habits and how they influence your energy levels, mood, and overall health. Are there any changes you can make to improve the quality of your diet and support your physical and mental well-being?

2. What Role Does Mindful Eating Play in Nourishing Your Body and Mind? Consider the importance of being present and mindful during meals. How does practicing mindful eating enhance your appreciation for food and promote a deeper connection with your body? How can you incorporate more mindfulness into your eating habits to support your journey of self-growth and holistic wellness?

24.
ORGANIZE EVERYTHING

There's a lot of energy getting wasted in deciding petty things during the day. We took care of it by planning the large chunks and visualizing the flow. Good!

I would like to point your attention to the things that take away energy without making any noise. It is possible that you may have noticed and still, you are unable to do anything. Don't laugh, I am about to tell you.

The clothes you're wearing. Let me explain. Don't do anything funny. Keep your clothes on. You must have noticed, some of the clothes make you feel uncomfortable in many ways. It could be itching or too tight or too loose, or just plain out of place for the occasion.

You need a good strategy to pick the most appropriate clothes (when you need clothes!) This is only to shut the distracting signals from the clothes and focus on the productive use of time. A whole new book on this topic some other day.

I will leave you to think about this and discuss it with your friends who are better in the clothing department. We humans first look at each other's clothes. Automatically, We decode the character in view before we interact with each other.

"Clear eyes are capable to see the path from the nearest to the farthest and all that is needed to be done along the way!"

It is very important that you present yourself in a way that doesn't rob you of your precious energy trying to present yourself as the top-notch personality that you think you are.

Begin from the nearest environment that needs rethinking and reorganizing. Clothes are extensions of your body. And after taking care of the body's needs, the next is what you put on. A good wardrobe is an asset far more worthy than you can imagine. Try it.

And let me add one more thing. If you carry a bag with you, as I do, turn it inside out once a week. There is so much lost and found stuff inside that you will laugh. And it is so much helpful to sort the stuff out for what is needed to be carried all the time and stuff that needs to be put away. And among everything, always carry a notebook and a pen. Use it for instant note-taking when an idea arrives.

I assure you it will turn out to be one of the best investments.

Exercises:

1. Wardrobe Audit: Set aside some time to go through your wardrobe and assess each item of clothing. Consider factors such as comfort, fit, and suitability for different occasions. Donate or discard any items that no longer serve you or make you feel uncomfortable. Organize your wardrobe in a way that makes it easy to find and access your clothes.

2. Bag Decluttering Session: Take a moment to empty out your bag or backpack and sort through its contents. Discard any items that are no longer needed or useful, such as old receipts or expired items. Organize the remaining items into designated compartments or pouches to keep them easily accessible and neatly arranged.

Questions to Ponder:

1. How Does Your Environment Impact Your Energy Levels? Reflect on how factors such as clothing choices and the organization of your belongings influence your overall well-being and productivity. Are there any changes you can make to optimize your environment and minimize distractions or discomfort?

2. What Role Does Organization Play in Supporting Your Daily Routine? Consider the importance of having a well-organized wardrobe and bag to streamline your daily activities. How does maintaining order in these areas contribute to a sense of control and efficiency in your everyday life? What strategies can you implement to enhance organization and minimize unnecessary stress or distractions?

25.
WHAT'S YOUR FUEL?

Five big senses. We consume through all five. It is not just the solid food that builds you. You are made of everything that you ingest. It is also called impressions.

Your attention throws the light, and through the same pipe of your attention the impressions walk in to you. Most of the time you are unaware.

You wonder why unaware? Because a part of you is not interested in what is coming in. This may happen for many reasons. Either the incoming information is average or you do not have curiosity for it, or you are not able to understand it or a part of you feels it is wrong to take in such information.

I shared in “A System without leakage”. Your attention pipe could be hijacked most of the time. And it brings in so much irrelevant information that the mind turns in to a dump yard over time. Reading this should help your mind awaken to this fact. By and by you will gain control over the pipe of attention.

The refinement of senses will help you pay attention to worthy subjects. (You are what you see, smell, touch, hear, taste)

This is like curating your art collection in the palace of mind. Imagine the beauty and peace you can bring in your mind if you stay awake.

You are what you see, smell, eat, hear, touch

Exercises:

1. Sensory Awareness Practice: Set aside some time each day to focus on each of your five senses individually. Close your eyes and pay attention to the sounds around you, then move on to focus on the sensations of touch, taste, smell, and finally, sight. Notice any subtle details or nuances you may have overlooked before. This practice can help you become more attuned to your surroundings and the information you absorb through your senses.

2. Impression Journaling: Keep a journal where you record the impressions you encounter throughout your day. This could include things you see, hear, read, or experience in any way. Reflect on how each impression makes you feel and whether it aligns with your values and goals. Use this journaling practice to become more mindful of the information you allow into your mind and its impact on your well-being.

Questions to Ponder:

1. What Are Your Primary Sources of Input? Reflect on the types of information and stimuli that dominate your daily life. Are there any sources of input that you rely on more heavily than others? How do these sources contribute to your overall mindset and well-being?

2. How Does Your Environment Shape Your Impressions? Consider how your physical environment influences the impressions you encounter on a daily basis. Are there any changes you can make to your environment to cultivate more positive and enriching experiences? How can you create a space that nurtures your growth and aligns with your values?

26.
½ HOUR MAGIC

You know what they say, time is money and if you're not careful, it can slip through your fingers like a greased up pig at a county fair. But fear not, my friends, for the solution to all of your time management woes is simple: divide your day into half hour slots.

Think about it, when you're faced with a whole 24 hours, it can be daunting and overwhelming. But when you break it down into little bite-sized chunks, it's like a buffet of time management opportunities. You can have a little bit of work, a little bit of play, and a little bit of "me time" all in one day. It's like having your cake and eating it too, except instead of cake, it's time.

And let's be real, who doesn't love a good buffet?

But it's not just about fitting everything in, it's about making sure that at the end of the day, you feel satisfied. And let's be real, there's nothing more satisfying than crossing off everything on your to-do list and still having time for a Netflix binge. With half hour slots, you can schedule in time for all the activities you enjoy, whether it's playing video games, going for a run, or even just taking a nap.

And let's not forget the added bonus of being able to schedule in "procrastination time." We've all been there, staring at a project and thinking "I'll do it later" only to realize later never comes. But with half hour slots, you can schedule in a designated procrastination time and finally cross that project off your list.

In short, dividing your day into half hour slots is like a magic wand for time management. It allows you to fit in all the activities you enjoy, makes you feel satisfied at the end of the day, and even includes a designated procrastination time. So go forth, my friends, and make the most of your time like a boss.

Exercises:

1. Half Hour Time Blocking: Take a blank sheet of paper or use a digital calendar app and divide your day into half-hour time slots from the moment you wake up until the moment you go to bed. Fill in each time slot with specific activities or tasks, ensuring you allocate time for work, leisure, self-care, and any other priorities. Stick to this schedule for a day and observe how it impacts your productivity and satisfaction.

2. Time Audit: Keep a journal for a week where you record how you spend each half-hour block of your day. Be honest and detailed about your activities, including how much time you spend on work, leisure, socializing, and other tasks. At the end of the week, review your journal and identify areas where you can optimize your time usage to align better with your goals and priorities.

Questions to Ponder:

1. What Are Your Time Management Challenges?
   Reflect on the areas of your life where you struggle to manage your time effectively. Are there specific tasks or activities that always seem to eat up more time than they should? How do you currently prioritize your time, and are there any changes you can make to improve your efficiency?

2. How Can Half Hour Time Blocking Benefit You?
   Consider how dividing your day into half-hour slots could positively impact your productivity, satisfaction, and

overall well-being. How might this approach help you balance work and leisure activities more effectively? What adjustments might you need to make to your current routine to incorporate this time management strategy?

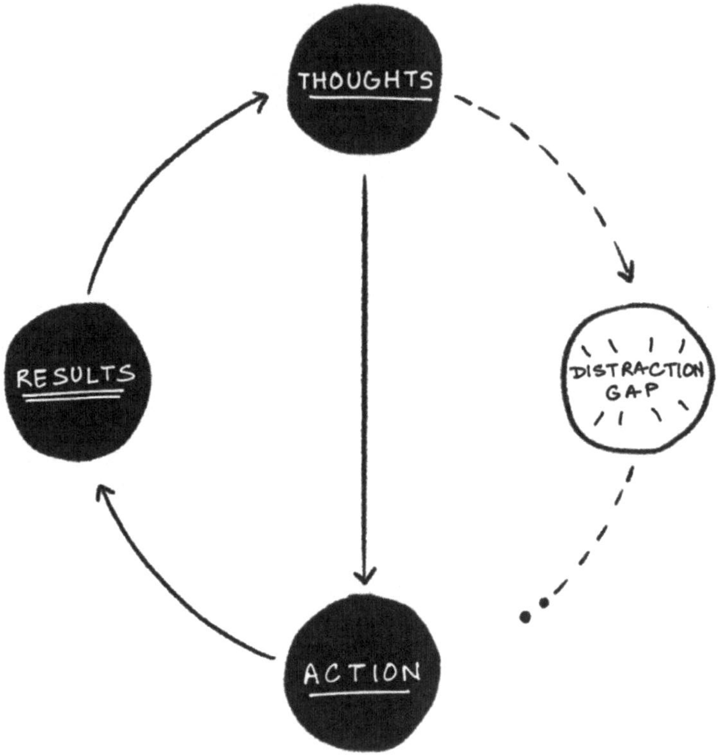
THOUGHTS
DISTRACTION GAP
RESULTS
ACTION

27.
THE GAP

Between the arrival of a thought and becoming your actions, there's a gap.

Your ignorance is hiding this gap. If you happen to spot the gap, it expands and then comes the creative part. You can design this beautiful gap to be an extremely productive asset.

There is a gap between the time we have a thought and the time we take action on it. This gap can be filled with a lot of things, such as fear, doubt, and procrastination.

However, if we can learn to be aware of this gap, we can use it to our advantage. The gap between thought and action is a space where creativity can flourish. It is a time when we can explore our options and come up with new ideas.

It is also a time when we can make mistakes and learn from them. If we can learn to embrace the gap between thought and action, we can use it to become more productive and creative. We can use this time to brainstorm new ideas, to plan our next steps, and to reflect on our progress.

Here are some tips for using the gap between thought and action to your advantage:

- Be aware of the gap. The first step is to be aware of the gap between thought and action. Once you are aware of it, you can start to pay attention to how you are filling it.
- Use the gap to brainstorm. The gap between thought and action is a great time to brainstorm new ideas. This is a time when you can let your mind wander and come up with new possibilities.

- Use the gap to plan. Once you have some new ideas, you can start to plan how you are going to implement them. This is a time to think about the steps you need to take and the resources you need.
- Use the gap to reflect. It is also important to use the gap between thought and action to reflect on your progress.

This is a time to think about what you have learned and how you can improve. The gap between thought and action is a powerful tool. If we can learn to use it to our advantage, we can become more productive and creative.

Exercises:

1. Mindfulness Practice: Throughout the day, set aside a few moments to consciously observe the gap between your thoughts and actions. Notice when a thought arises and before you act upon it. Take a deep breath and use this moment of awareness to consider your options before proceeding with action. Practice this exercise regularly to cultivate mindfulness in navigating the gap.

2. Gap Journaling: Keep a journal or notebook handy and jot down instances where you become aware of the gap between your thoughts and actions. Reflect on what you were thinking and how you chose to respond or act. Identify any patterns or tendencies in how you fill this gap and brainstorm alternative approaches to make it more productive and creative.

Questions to Ponder:

1. What Typically Fills Your Gap Between Thought and Action? Reflect on your usual response or behavior when you encounter the gap between having a thought and taking action. Are you often influenced by fear, doubt, or procrastination? How might recognizing and altering these tendencies impact your productivity and creativity?

2. How Can You Optimize the Gap for Growth and Improvement? Consider how you can leverage the gap between thought and action as a space for personal growth and development. What strategies can you implement to make this gap more conducive to brainstorming, planning, and reflection? How might embracing this gap enhance your ability to navigate challenges and pursue your goals with clarity and intention?

28.
THE FIRST PRINCIPLE

I am talking about meditation. Well, there are no strict principles of meditation as such. I just made it up to sound pompous. But let me tell you a secret. Meditation happens. You can not DO meditation. It is a shortcoming of language. Meditation means a lot of things. One of them means "to arrive at an uncluttered state of mind".

And the system we went through helps to reach that point. We made better relations with all our split personalities. We did that by accepting them for what they are and giving them due attention, time, and energy. Not only that, but we made all the hanging and dangling parts within us into a single, unified individual.

Now, when you sit to meditate, you may expect silence in the mind. That is actually silence “from the mind”. By and by, it is going to be so much more natural than ever before. Give it a shot. Again, begin softly and sneakily by sitting for just a few minutes, and you'll start to get the hang of it. This is purely to become a better thinker. The simple logic here is that the muscles perform better when given proper rest. Meditation is one such name for giving good and active rest to thinking faculty. Active, because you are fully awake. You are still not actively thinking, but just being an observer. Sounds amazing, yeah?

Trying to meditate without becoming undivided is futile. And still, that is how nature prepares us. You may have to face all the suppressed personalities demanding attention.

"Suppressing your dark side is like holding the door to keep the devil out. The devil is persistent. You grow tired. Finally, the Door collapses!"

The one who has made friends with all the devils within will not be frightened. I mean, now you know the reason why you are reluctant to try meditation. A part of you wants to keep suppressing your dark side.

The smart strategy is to form an alliance with the dark side art in you. This is the path to becoming united. The formidable force of a person that utilizes the right kind of inner team member. In every game of life, you will let the right part lead, depending on the situation. Something like X-Men. Solid analogy, yeah?

It's a wild world. Every sane parent who has survived the forces that contaminate the minds to become a blind slave to the authorities of all sorts would agree. They want their child to accept all her traits as an arsenal for the appropriate occasion. Life is unpredictable and everything changes, fast!

You are trained to hate certain parts of you because it isn't good for others who conspire to claim authority over you.
Once you realize this, the fragments in you naturally begin to unite. A wholesomeness begins to appear within. This is your moment of celebration. Because you have discovered the secret to multiplying your forces. This will be a great start to redesigning the remaining life with a fresh new start! (..Music!)

Exercises:

1. Inner Alliance Meditation: Set aside a few minutes each day to sit in a quiet space and practice meditation. As you close your eyes, imagine yourself surrounded by all the different aspects of your personality, both light and dark. Visualize each aspect as a distinct entity within you, and then work on fostering a sense of unity and cooperation among them. Allow yourself to become the observer of these inner dynamics without judgment or resistance, aiming to cultivate a harmonious inner alliance.

2. Shadow Work Journaling: Start a journal dedicated to exploring your shadow self—the aspects of your personality that you may have suppressed or disowned. Reflect on any traits or tendencies that you find difficult to accept or acknowledge within yourself. Write about your experiences, emotions, and insights as you delve deeper into understanding and embracing these aspects of your psyche. Use this journaling practice as a tool for integrating your shadow self and fostering greater self-awareness.

Questions to Ponder:

1. What Parts of Yourself Have You Been Suppressing or Rejecting? Take some time to reflect on the different aspects of your personality that you may have been avoiding or denying. Consider why you might have developed resistance towards these parts of yourself and how acknowledging and accepting them could contribute to your overall well-being and growth.

2. How Can You Foster Inner Unity and Cooperation Among Your Various Personality Aspects? Think about ways in which you can nurture a sense of harmony and collaboration among the different facets of your being. What practices or strategies can you implement to encourage mutual understanding and support within yourself? How might embracing all parts of yourself contribute to a more integrated and empowered sense of self?

29.
[20 / 80]

20 % energy spent because of routine on set playlist (automatic) 80 % energy available to think clearer.

This will bring a smile to your face. And it will come after you automate the routine tasks with all the probable distractions in the scheduled slot. The energy build-up will put you into the driving seat. The mood uplifts on its own.

I call this 80/20. The details of a planned day will need 20 percent energy. A large chunk of 80 percent of energy becomes available for building something outstanding.

Ever wondered why you couldn't achieve many of those new year's resolutions and other targets? The energy reservoir was getting depleted by distractions. It was stealing most of it, every waking hour of your day.

Well, there was little room for observation in the middle of that chaotic life. There was no room to give any deeper thought to searching for a remedy to overcome the situation. And it stays difficult when we try to solve the whole thing all at once.

"Deep Thinking needs a lot of energy and a very clear mind. It only gets easier when you have a plan!"

The easier route is to work part by part, bird by bird. And in no time we can come to this 20/80 stage. All the regular activities are taken care of well within 20 percent of energy. After this, a large lot of remaining energy is at your disposal to create a fresh new timeline!

And now we have a plan. So keep working on it every day to make it a little better than the previous day. And soon you will be teaching this to other less fortunate ones who didn't get this book! I mean..

Exercises:

1. Routine Automation Exercise: Take some time to identify the routine tasks in your daily life that consume a significant amount of your energy. This could include activities like meal preparation, commuting, or checking emails. Once you've identified these tasks, brainstorm ways to automate or streamline them to require less mental effort. For example, you could create meal plans or set up email filters to organize your inbox. Implement these automation strategies and observe how they free up more of your mental energy for other endeavors.

2. Energy Audit: Conduct an energy audit of your typical day by tracking how you allocate your energy throughout various activities. Make note of the tasks or situations that drain your energy the most, as well as those that leave you feeling energized or fulfilled. Use this information to identify opportunities for optimizing your energy usage and maximizing your productivity. Consider adjustments you can make to better align your energy expenditure with your priorities and goals.

Questions to Ponder:

1. What Routine Tasks Could You Automate to Save Mental Energy? Reflect on the repetitive tasks that you perform regularly and consider how you could automate or streamline them to require less cognitive effort. How might implementing automation strategies improve your overall efficiency and effectiveness in managing your daily responsibilities?

2. How Can You Optimize Your Energy Usage to Support Your Goals? Think about how you currently allocate your mental energy throughout the day and whether it aligns with your aspirations and objectives. Are there any adjustments you could make to prioritize tasks that contribute most to your personal or professional growth? How might optimizing your energy usage help you achieve a greater sense of fulfillment and accomplishment?

30.
MEDITATION IS FISHING

You may have heard that fishing is a meditation. Let me reverse this idea and present a beautiful model for your everyday practice.

After the system "Contract with Self" takes off, spare a few minutes in the less crowded slot of time. 20 minutes is good to start with. You are free to increase the number of minutes as you get comfortable with the practice of this new sort of meditation.

Imagine you are fishing. The water is slowly getting calm as the minutes flow by. There is also a shelf beside you with numbered compartments. This is to store the thought fishes that you capture in the session.

Where are thought-fishes? Oh, the thought is floating like fishes. Notice some of the persistent ones returning into your field of vision repeatedly. Look at them carefully. Keep your notebook handy. If the thought is urgent plus important and needs good follow-up, write it down immediately. Return to the thought fishing meditation.

The others option is to learn a memory trick to stow away the thought safely in the shelf we imagined in the beginning. I give you five slots. One-Sun, Two-Shoe, Three-Tree, Four-Door, Five-Hive.

"There are many rules for designing a meditation technique. The Most important one is, It should work instantly!"

These are not just rhyming words, but our keys to tagging the thoughts and keep on the shelves. Associate the first thought that comes up, with Sun. The second thought with shoes and so on. Make a little story with the associated word, and the thought will stop to reoccur. It is like attaching a free electron to make the molecule stable. Elementary, my dear Watson!

Let me tell you how you are ahead of most meditators. Start practicing fishing meditation after your daily system of "Contract with Self" is up and running. Most of the loose and dangling fragments of routine life are put in their right places. There should be only important and weighty thoughts coming to you for your attention. Now, this is a solid strategy to go in search of thoughts that need resolution.

Most old-school meditators are fretting to run away from thoughts and failure. Every time. Invariably. Most of them aren't bold enough to confess or even conscious enough to notice the failure. Here, we are boldly going where no one has gone even before. I mean, almost no one. In search of the lost thoughts so that they don't fall on us in the inappropriate time slot. Now that is outstandingly smart! 😎

Exercises:

1. Thought-Fishing Meditation Practice: Set aside 20 minutes in your daily schedule to practice thought-fishing meditation. Find a quiet and comfortable space where you can sit undisturbed. Close your eyes and imagine yourself by a tranquil lake, with each thought appearing as a fish swimming by. Use the numbered compartments in your mental shelf to store and organize the thoughts that arise during the meditation session. Practice capturing and tagging each thought with a mnemonic device, such as associating them with the numbers one through five. Reflect on how this practice helps you cultivate a sense of mental clarity and organization.

2. Memory Association Game: Create a memory association game using the mnemonic devices introduced in the meditation practice. Write down a list of common objects or concepts and assign each one to a number from one to five (e.g., sun, shoe, tree, door, hive). Then, challenge yourself to recall the associated item for each number without referring back to your list. Practice this game regularly to strengthen your memory and cognitive skills.

Questions to Ponder:

1. How Does the Fishing Meditation Technique Help You Manage Your Thoughts? Reflect on your experience with the thought-fishing meditation practice. How does the imagery of fishing and the use of numbered compartments assist you in capturing and organizing your thoughts? What benefits do you notice in terms of mental clarity and focus as you engage in this meditation technique?

2. What Strategies Can You Use to Improve Your Memory Association Skills? Consider how you can enhance your ability to associate thoughts with mnemonic devices like the numbered compartments in the fishing meditation practice. Are there any additional memory techniques or exercises you could incorporate into your daily routine to strengthen your memory and cognitive function? How might improving your memory association skills benefit other areas of your life, beyond meditation?

31.
OCEAN MEDITATION

You have everything within you. And you are in everything. It is an endless and infinite loop. You may disagree. And your disagreement is part of this infinity.

Everything you feel, see, hear touch, think, experience, and imagine is part of this infinity. Like an endless ocean, the whole is complete. There is nothing to do and nowhere to reach. It is all here and now. Big words? Let me serve it in a cup to you.

Sit in a place where you will not be easily disturbed. And yes, put away that mobile phone! Make space for at least a few minutes when you start this practice. Any time of the day is good. The start and end of the day have some added magic to this game. Do it as many times as you can. This is medicinal, no kidding.

Imagine, you are an ocean. Endless. Borderless. All the weathers are within you. The storms and the calm. The high wind and the stagnant breeze. The blue and black waters. All the instincts are part of you. All the emotions are part of you. All the thoughts and ideas are part of you. That resistance to sitting for this practice is part of you. The logic in you shouting loud to get the hell out of this nonsense is part of you.

Just welcome everything. They are all your waves, And they come to you in different sizes and shapes, and forces.

"Breathe like an ocean. Let everything become part of you. Stay open and warm. Keep expanding!"

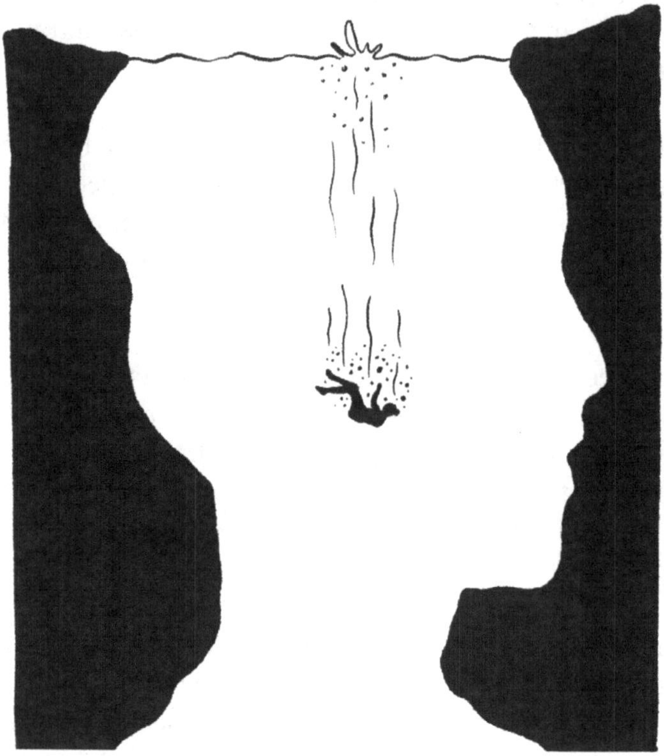

There will be hidden resistance to that obvious resistance of practicing meditation. Yeah, pause and read again. You get it. Let that to be part of you.

There will be a desire to fight certain waves. Now you are creating waves to fight the waves. Cute! It is all ok. Let it happen. There will be sudden reflexes to push away certain memories. Step back in your mind and include that too. Keep expanding as an ocean. Space is no limitation. We are playing the game of infinity.

Feel free to move your body. As long as you are alive, there will be movements. No need to be rigid. Stay flexible to scratch, yawn and make burping noises if that makes you feel better. If part of the body gets numb, move softly to adjust. Why am I giving such advice? Believe me, these questions will come when you practice. And I have given such simple answers to people in my workshops.

Exercises:

1. Ocean Visualization Meditation: Find a quiet and comfortable space where you can sit or lie down without being disturbed. Close your eyes and take several deep breaths to relax your body and mind. Imagine yourself as an expansive ocean, with endless depths and vastness. Visualize the ebb and flow of waves within you, representing your thoughts, emotions, and sensations. Allow yourself to fully experience the sensations of being the ocean, embracing everything that arises within you without judgment or resistance. Practice this meditation for at least 5-10 minutes, gradually increasing the duration as you become more comfortable with the practice.

2. Journaling Reflection: After completing the ocean visualization meditation, take a few minutes to journal

about your experience. Reflect on the sensations, emotions, and thoughts that arose during the meditation. Did you notice any resistance or challenges? How did you respond to these obstacles? What insights or revelations did you gain from the practice? Write down any observations or reflections that come to mind, allowing yourself to explore your inner landscape with curiosity and openness.

Questions to Ponder:

1. How Does the Concept of Being an Ocean Resonate With You? Reflect on the metaphor of being an ocean and embracing all aspects of yourself, including thoughts, emotions, and sensations. How does this perspective shift your understanding of self-awareness and acceptance? In what ways can you apply the principles of openness and expansiveness in your daily life to cultivate a sense of inner peace and wholeness?

2. What Strategies Can You Use to Embrace Resistance and Challenges? Consider how you can adopt a mindset of openness and flexibility when faced with resistance or challenges during meditation or other self-growth practices. How can you reframe obstacles as opportunities for growth and learning? Are there any specific techniques or approaches that resonate with you for navigating resistance and embracing the full spectrum of your experiences?

32.
IF YOU ARE ALIVE

That is one difference between being dead and being alive. You don't know what dead feels like, that's all. But you do know what being alive? is like. Think about it for a minute. You might argue that breathing thinking feeling makes you feel like you are alive. No, I'm not saying that. I want you to focus on pure being alive.

You might feel like a piece of background music playing deep underneath. Or a very sophisticated, silent machinery, working inside. Isn't it amazing how the heart keeps going, and you don't know how? Your hair keeps growing, and you have no idea how you do it. It's all happening on its own. We label things and assume that we understand. In reality, we have no idea.

Give a little rest to hopes and dreams and inspiration for a moment and pause. Just feel happy and contented for being alive because someday you will not be alive. This is a rare opportunity that you are reading this, and you are alive. Feel gratitude for this opportunity.

The mind will do its part while you are feeling alive. Let that be part of the music. If you feel hungry, or thirsty, let that be a gift of a machine that makes you feel alive.

Whenever you get time, come back to this space of aliveness. Do it as many times as you can in a day. This is like giving air to the fire. The flower that creates life.

You do not need much time or space or anything specific. Mindfully, comeback to yourself. This will be a quick and easy reset to the chaos of daily life.

Exercises:

1. Aliveness Meditation: Find a quiet and comfortable space where you can sit or lie down without distractions. Close your eyes and take a few deep breaths to center yourself. Focus your attention on the sensation of being alive. Notice the beating of your heart, the rhythm of your breath, and any other signs of vitality within your body. Allow yourself to simply be present in this moment of aliveness, without judgment or analysis. Practice this meditation for a few minutes each day, gradually increasing the duration as you become more attuned to the sensation of being alive.

2. Gratitude Journaling: Set aside a few minutes each day to reflect on the gift of life and express gratitude for the experience of being alive. Take out a journal or notebook and write down three things you are grateful for in relation to your aliveness. These could be simple things like the feeling of sunshine on your skin, the taste of your favorite food, or the sound of laughter. Cultivate an attitude of appreciation for the small moments of aliveness that enrich your day.

Questions to Ponder:

1. What Does Being Alive Mean to You? Reflect on the concept of aliveness and what it means to you personally. How do you experience the sensation of being alive in your everyday life? Are there particular activities or moments that make you feel especially connected to your sense of aliveness? Explore how your understanding of aliveness influences your perspective on life and the world around you.

2. How Can You Cultivate a Deeper Sense of Aliveness? Consider ways in which you can cultivate a deeper awareness of your own aliveness and vitality. Are there mindfulness practices or rituals that resonate with you for reconnecting to the present moment and embracing the gift of life? How can you integrate moments of gratitude and appreciation into your daily routine to foster a greater sense of aliveness and fulfillment?

33.
REFLECT

The unexamined life is not worth living." - Socrates This part sounds like poetry. It will be challenging when you practice reflection on your past 24 hours. Give it a try now, and you will realize why I said that. Come on, try it. Just start from this morning, the moment you opened your eyes and the arrival of the first thought. Get the picture? Ok.. Ok.. Read on!

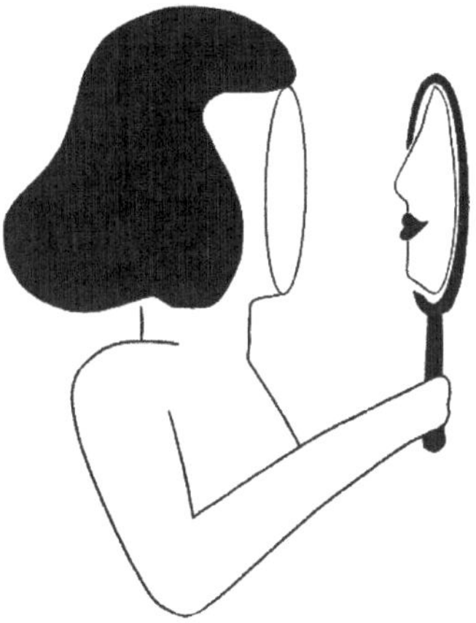

This is the most important task I suggest you do every day. You may do it before going to sleep or first thing in the morning if you are too tired or drunk to reflect at night. I know! Glide through your entire day in as much detail as possible, and the grove will get groovier. There is juice here, and you need to develop the taste for this one.

In our routine life, we function like half zombies or bad robots. Why Because that is how most of us are designed by the complicated forces of nature (sorry nature lovers!) Not your fault. Humans have intellect, but it is hard to use it most of the time. And this is so because of many factors pulling us from all directions.

The remedy is to find quiet time before bed. Time to look at how we lived through the day. A lot of details will become clearer where you were unable to give your attention.

"Reflecting on your last 24 hours is like coming to full circle, retracing your steps and then stepping upwards in your spiral of growth."

These could be tiny events and happenings which were not processed completely. There are many valid reasons for this. This is how excess baggage is created in the subconscious mind. Part reason why we live as half zombies.

In the absence of deliberate reflection at the end of the day, such tiny threads of unprocessed stuff pile up. Eventually, it becomes a serious dumpster. Most of us are carrying a brain almost like a broken garage truck. No space here for anything fresh. And even if you bring in something fresh, you can imagine the consequences, ya?

Between you and me, reflection is just pouring the water of attention on the area which was left dry in the rush of the day.

And this will be your winning edge in a world rushing madly not knowing where to. A lot of gains can be ripped by reflection because it will awaken you to mend your ways in the future. It will make you better at being more aware of everything you have been doing habitually and unconsciously. Make small changes organically as you go forward in the future. Everything will begin to transform.

Exercises:

1. Daily Reflection Journal: Set aside time at the end of each day to reflect on your experiences over the past 24 hours. Take out a journal or notebook and write down key events,

interactions, and emotions you encountered throughout the day. Reflect on how these experiences made you feel and what insights you gained from them. Use this journaling practice as an opportunity to cultivate self-awareness and identify areas for growth.

2. Mindful Review Meditation: Find a quiet space where you can sit comfortably without distractions. Close your eyes and take a few deep breaths to center yourself. Then, mentally review your day from start to finish, observing each moment without judgment. Notice any thoughts, feelings, or sensations that arise as you recall your experiences. Allow yourself to fully immerse in the process of reflection, embracing whatever arises with curiosity and compassion.

Questions to Ponder:

1. What Patterns or Themes Do You Notice in Your Daily Reflections? As you engage in daily reflection, pay attention to any recurring patterns or themes that emerge in your experiences. Are there certain habits, behaviors, or thought patterns that consistently show up in your reflections? How do these patterns contribute to your overall sense of well-being and personal growth? Reflecting on these insights can help you make intentional changes to enhance your life.

2. How Can You Use Reflection to Guide Your Future Actions? Consider how you can leverage the insights gained from your daily reflections to inform your future actions and decisions. Are there specific areas of your life where you would like to see improvement or growth? How can you apply the lessons learned from your reflections to create positive change moving forward? By using reflection as a tool for self-discovery and self-improvement, you can cultivate a greater sense of clarity and purpose in your daily life.

34. WHY DIDN'T YOU TELL ME THIS EARLIER?

Ever felt like your thoughts, feelings, and ideas are like playful kids in your mind, your inner city? In this chapter, we'll explore how these inner musings behave and how we share them with others.

Imagine your mind as a busy playground, filled with colorful characters—your thoughts, feelings, and ideas—all trying to get attention. Sometimes, they need a little push to come out and play with the world.

There is Hide-and-Seek of Ideas going on all the time. Have you ever looked for an idea, only for it to pop up unexpectedly? It's like chasing after a group of excited kids—they're hard to catch! But when they finally appear, it feels like finding hidden treasure.

Just like shy kids, our thoughts and feelings can be hesitant to leave our minds. They want to find people who will understand them before they come out to play. Deciding who to share our thoughts and feelings with can be tough. It's like inviting people to a party—you want to choose the right guests. But don't worry, figuring it out is part of the fun!

Do we need permission to share our thoughts and feelings? It's a tricky question, but maybe what matters most is whether we feel ready to share. The Bold

Eventually, our thoughts, feelings, and ideas become brave enough to come out and meet new people. They're excited to share their stories with anyone who will listen.

Sharing our inner thoughts, feelings, and ideas is like going on a fun adventure. Whether they come out quietly or loudly, essential is to celebrate their bravery and enjoy the journey together. Think about the playful nature of the mind and the joy of sharing our innermost thoughts with others.

And that sharing will happen when the thoughts have grown up to walk out in the world boldly or when there is a warm and loving person with whom the thought would like to mingle because there is an air of safety about that person.

So next time someone puts you on the spot saying "why didn't you tell me this earlier?" You can share the insights you gained from this chapter. No need to feel guilt or shame. You may rather psyche them with this philosophical truth. What say?

35.
AN INDIVIDUAL

An individual is the one who is able to think independently. Just giving undivided attention brings light to the subject, any subject. The obstacle is all the surrounding noise that enters within and over a long period starts to feel as if it is normal. Well, it is not. One must wake up to stand against this and find ways to a better self.

A wholesome person is like a strong team. In sports, a strong team is one that has a large variety of players. Each player respects all the other players. There is no enemy within, and the leader changes as per the mode of the game.

You must understand the divisions within your personality. And still, all these divisions must work in harmony and stand together in support of one another, unquestionably.

Upon well-understood, practice of contract with self brings one to the point of clarity. Here, one knows the right timing to bring up the right personality type. And let this personality trait act as the lead character to play the role at its best.

There remain lesser cracks in the inner structure. And wherever a clear crack appears, it is given due attention to find out why it happened. Acceptance of this crack will happen by understanding its origins. Warmly include this new character within you. Accept it as part of the crew of characters residing within. This will make the whole self much stronger as it is not-a-divided self, but a multiplied self. I am sure now you can imagine how powerful you are designed to be, isn't it?

"A unified individual is the one who has no enemies within."

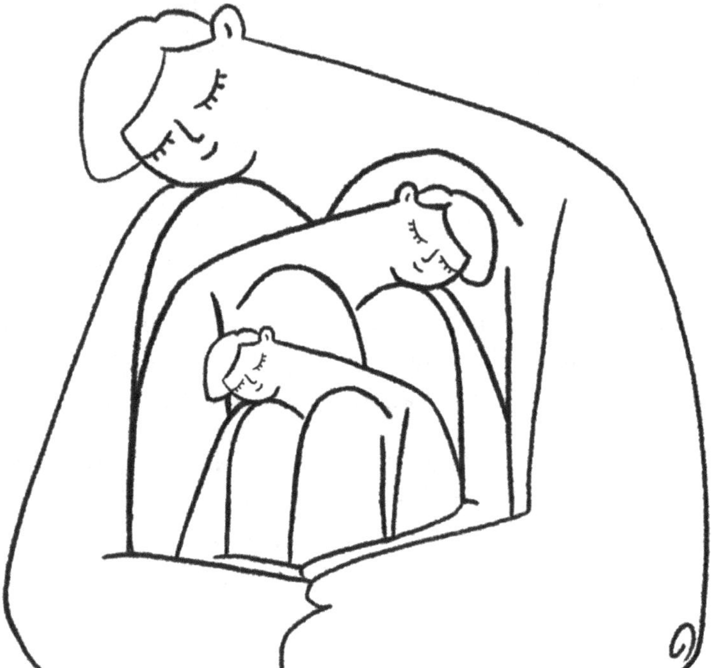

The key to growth and freedom is to understand why you were a bundle of splits. All sorts of authority figures have been at it since the beginning of time. This is why one becomes biased against oneself in a due course of time and finds the enemy within.

Strange! If you're not your own best friend, how can you be that to others? If you're not happy within, how can you make others happy? Umm, you can pretend, but it will just add to your burden and excess baggage on your mind and body.

A few noticeable changes. You will enjoy looking for more lost splits existing within. It will get easier to bring them too into the unified model. The energy drain begins to reduce. Now the free energy becomes available to the brain. This naturally works to generate fresh new, innovative and insightful thinking.

There are many books on the subject of how to think. They may help to get a better orientation and improve the worldview and also how the world works. Yes, we think we know, but there's a lot more to learn that can astonish the one who is ready to learn more.

The best gift you can give yourself is the ability to think multidimensionally. And keep upgrading your understanding of yourself and the world at large. The unbiased thinking that keeps re-evaluating itself is an unstoppable force. And this will create a path to healing from old wounds. This will help with the creation of physical, mental, and financial wealth and yes, happiness!

Exercises:

1. Inner Harmony Visualization: Find a quiet and comfortable space where you can sit or lie down without distractions. Close your eyes and take a few deep breaths to relax your body and mind. Then, visualize yourself as a team of players in a sports game. Each player represents a different aspect of your personality or character traits. Take note of how each player interacts with the others and whether there is any conflict or harmony among them. As you visualize this inner team, focus on fostering a sense of unity and cooperation among all the players, recognizing that each one has a valuable role to play in your life.

2. Personality Integration Journaling: Set aside time each day to journal about the different aspects of your personality or character traits. Reflect on how each trait contributes to your overall identity and behavior. Identify any conflicts or divisions within yourself and explore the underlying reasons for these divisions. Write down your thoughts and feelings about integrating these aspects of yourself into a more cohesive and unified whole. Use this journaling practice as an opportunity to deepen your understanding of yourself and promote self-growth and self-acceptance.

Questions to Ponder:

1. What Are the Different Aspects of Your Personality?
   Take some time to reflect on the various traits, qualities, and characteristics that make up your personality. Are there certain traits that dominate your behavior, or do you exhibit a wide range of traits depending on the situation? How do these different aspects of your personality interact with each other, and are there any conflicts or tensions between them? Exploring the complexity of your

personality can help you gain insights into your inner world and foster greater self-awareness.

2. How Can You Cultivate Inner Harmony and Unity? Consider ways in which you can foster greater harmony and unity among the different aspects of your personality. Are there certain practices or techniques that resonate with you, such as mindfulness, meditation, or self-reflection? How can you create a supportive and nurturing environment within yourself, where all parts of your being feel valued and respected? Reflecting on these questions can help you develop strategies for integrating your diverse personality traits into a more cohesive and unified whole.

36.
WATCH THE GAP

To be happy, you have to watch the gap. The gap between what you have and what you want. Accept the gap. Accept the fact that you are unhappy because you do not have what you want. This is nature's way to put you on the path to achieve higher goals.

Taking advice like "one should be content with what one has" will only add to the pain. You need to be honest with yourself. If you have desire, give your attention to it. Write it in our journal. Maybe your attention is all it needs.

Expand your field of vision and include all the thoughts surrounding your desires. For every situation, there might be a cluster of thoughts. Watch your mind when your partner is in conflict with you. You want to change your partner's behavior. You have an alternate plan in your mind how the other should talk and behave. Then you might get thoughts about accepting your partner as the nature has decided to create.

The only thing possible in those moments is to observe all the thoughts about how the situation should be and how it actually is. And the gap in between. It usually takes time. Practice stepping back in your mind and keep including all the thoughts in your field of vision. It is futile to fight the thoughts. And if a fight happens, include that too in your field of vision.

The divided mind stays in pain for either of two reasons. One reason is, the mind rushes to the future to imagine the desired situation. The other reason is, the mind curses the present situation.

Your ability to watch the gap will help you witness the big picture.

Watch and include everything that you can watch. Usually it is more pain from thoughts you are unable to watch properly.

Exercises:

1. Mindful Gap Observation: Set aside a few minutes each day to practice mindful gap observation. Find a quiet and comfortable space where you can sit undisturbed. Close your eyes and take a few deep breaths to center yourself. Then, bring your attention to the present moment and observe any gaps between what you have and what you want. Notice any feelings of discontent or longing that arise, and simply observe them without judgment. Allow yourself to fully experience the gap without trying to change it. After a few minutes, gently bring your awareness back to the present moment and open your eyes.

2. Desire Journaling: Start a journal where you can explore your desires and the gaps between what you have and what you want. Take some time each day to write down your desires, big or small, and reflect on the thoughts and emotions that accompany them. Notice any patterns or themes that emerge, and consider how your desires influence your sense of happiness and fulfillment. Use this

journaling practice as a tool for self-reflection and self-awareness, allowing yourself to explore the gap between your current reality and your desired outcomes.

Questions to Ponder:

1. What Are Your Deepest Desires? Take some time to reflect on your most profound desires and aspirations. What do you truly want in life, and why is it important to you? Are there any recurring themes or patterns in your desires, and what do they reveal about your values and priorities? Exploring your deepest desires can help you gain clarity about what truly matters to you and guide your actions towards fulfilling those desires.

2. How Do You Navigate the Gap Between Reality and Expectations? Consider how you typically respond to the gaps between your current reality and your desired outcomes. Do you tend to resist or reject the present moment, longing for a different reality? Or do you accept and embrace the gap, recognizing it as a natural part of the journey towards growth and fulfillment? Reflecting on your approach to navigating the gap can help you develop strategies for cultivating greater acceptance, resilience, and happiness in your life.

37.
LET EMOTIONS REACH THE BODY

Emotions are chemical cocktails manufactured in the brain. The effects of these cocktails are felt in the body. Heart space is one such area.

Emotions we call positive are Gratitude, love, celebration, and such. And there are bitter emotions like sadness, hatred, revenge, and jealousy. I don't enjoy the effect of negative emotions most of the time. That is why I keep looking for an escape. By escaping, I meant I tend to postpone the process.

When I decide to stay with the feeling creating pain in my body part, I am allowing it to dissipate. It is not possible to know the duration of time the pain will stay or be gone. All I can choose to do sometimes is to stay and let it be.

Alternatively, when I am resistant to feeling pain in the body, I hold the cocktail in my brain. This makes the brain environment toxic.

This fear of not being able to handle the pain in the body is false. It is just a habit of mental constipation. To not let the cocktail pass through to the body. And all the while we complain of this pain not leaving the brain.

It is like holding on to something tightly and at the same time expecting it to be released at the same time.

A clear observation will bring an understanding. The grip will loosen and the flow of cocktails from the brain to the body will happen. It will feel like going back to your true nature. And it is your nature. This is how the cycle will become healthy again.

Our intellect makes us hold emotions tightly. We overthink how to express it, and it piles up. The dump yard of old emotions. Society is not very open to receiving you with positive or negative emotions pouring down your ears.

We want to look good in front of people. We think showing only what they want to see will be a good strategy. So the front facade is clean and attractive. The backyard is upside down.

Your body is like a mischievous mime, silently conveying messages that your mind struggles to interpret. From subtle sensations to not-so-subtle symptoms, it's constantly trying to communicate with you—whether you're paying attention or not.

Ever found yourself in a relationship that feels like it's gone past its expiration date? Your body knows it's time to hit the road long before your mind catches on. Chronic colds, stomach aches, and that gnawing feeling in your gut are just a few of the subtle hints it drops. Listen up, folks—your body's got your back!

On the flip side, when something is truly worth pursuing, your body sends signals of pure joy and excitement. That electric feeling coursing through your veins? It's your body's way of saying, **"Keep chasing that dream, you magnificent beast!"**

"Embrace Your Feelings"

Sometimes, your body knows you need a break long before you do. Exhaustion becomes your body's not-so-subtle way of saying, **"Slow down, buddy! Rest is the key to unraveling life's mysteries."**

Ever had that heart-pounding, hair-raising moment when you just knew something wasn't right? Your body's built-in alarm system kicks into high gear, sending adrenaline coursing through your veins like a herd of stampeding wildebeests. Pay attention, folks—your body's trying to save your bacon!

When you find yourself in the presence of someone who feels like home, your body lets out a sigh of relief. Relaxed breathing, feelings of peace, and a profound sense of appreciation—your body's way of saying, **"Stay awhile, friend. You're safe here."**

Trust your gut, they say. And for good reason! That sinking feeling in the pit of your stomach? It's your body's way of saying, **"Danger, Will Robinson! Something's fishy!"**

Grief weighs heavy on the soul, but your body knows just what you need. It's okay to take it slow, to be kind to yourself, and to let those tears flow freely. Your body's there to remind you that healing takes time.

You know this already. Intrinsically. I get it. That is why I shared this idea of a closed-door meeting with the self. At least in solitude, open up and let the suppressed emotions pour out. Meet them. Greet them. Talk to them. It will be a celebration of old friends reuniting. Why? Because emotions are your true friends.

Exercises:

1. Body Scan Meditation: Find a comfortable and quiet space where you can sit or lie down undisturbed. Close your eyes and take a few deep breaths to center yourself. Start by bringing your awareness to your feet and slowly move your attention upward, scanning each part of your body. Notice any areas of tension, discomfort, or sensation. As you encounter these sensations, try to breathe into them and allow them to soften and release. Pay special attention to any emotions that arise as you scan your body, and notice how they manifest physically. Practice this body scan meditation regularly to deepen your connection between your emotions and physical sensations.

2. Emotion Release Journaling: Set aside some time each day to journal about your emotions and their physical manifestations. Reflect on the emotions you experienced throughout the day and how they affected your body. Write down any physical sensations or discomfort you noticed, as well as the corresponding emotions. Use this journaling practice as an opportunity to explore the connection between your emotional and physical states, and to identify any patterns or triggers that may be contributing to your experiences.

Questions to Ponder:

1. How Do You Typically Handle Negative Emotions? Reflect on your usual response to negative emotions such as sadness, anger, or fear. Do you tend to suppress or avoid these emotions, or do you allow yourself to fully experience them? Consider how your approach to negative emotions may impact your overall well-being and ability to process and release them.

2. What Are Some Strategies for Allowing Emotions to Flow Through Your Body? Think about different techniques or practices that you can use to facilitate the healthy flow of emotions from your brain to your body. Are there any mindfulness exercises, relaxation techniques, or self-care practices that resonate with you? Experiment with incorporating these strategies into your daily routine to see how they affect your emotional and physical well-being.

38.
SIMPLIFY

The infiltration of media has done one funny thing. And this thing has entered into our minds and lifestyles. Complexity. Most of us believe that complex brand names, complex music, complex clothing, complex conversations make us look so cool. If things are presented with simplicity, it might not get higher status.

It is one thing to weave a complex and rich story plot. It is another thing to create such complex structure in our minds. We present things to ourselves in complex ways. We try to hide stuff from our own selves. This creates a dark and heavy subconscious mind.

Be transparent to at lease yourself. The thoughts transiting your mind needs to be observed. In as simple way as possible. Include them in the light of your attention. Hiding or looking away from thighs just create a complex entanglement is going to be a lot of homework! And you don't like homework, right?

All that you receive, chew it properly and simplify. For your self and others. And writing is a fantastic tool to simplify thought.

Imagine a house so complex that even the owner gets lost in it. That house is your very own mind. Build it in such a way that you know its geography. And that help you use it to the fullest capacity.

Keeping it in your head:

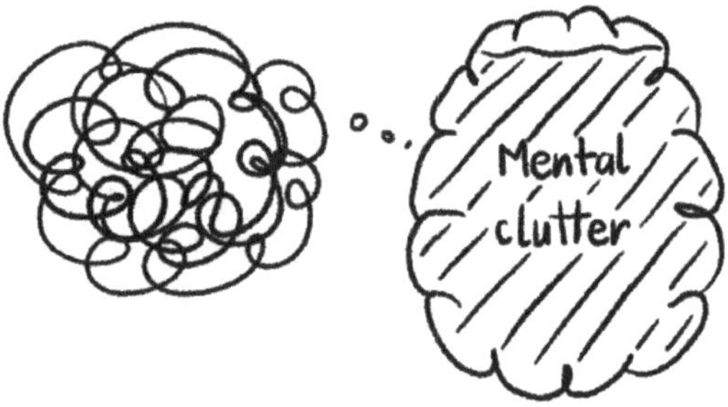

Writing it down:

Exercises:

1. Stream-of-Consciousness Writing: Set a timer for 10-15 minutes and begin writing continuously without pausing or editing. Let your thoughts flow freely onto the page, even if they seem disjointed or nonsensical at first. Don't worry about grammar or punctuation – the goal is to capture your stream of consciousness. This exercise can help you untangle complex thoughts and gain clarity on your innermost feelings and ideas.

Questions to Ponder:

1. How Does Complexity Impact Your Life? Reflect on the ways in which complexity manifests in your daily life, whether it's in your thoughts, behaviors, relationships, or environment. Consider how complexity may contribute to feelings of overwhelm, confusion, or stress, and whether simplifying certain aspects of your life could lead to greater ease and clarity.

2. What Are Some Strategies for Simplifying Your Mindset? Think about practical steps you can take to simplify your mindset and approach to life. Are there any habits, routines, or activities that you could simplify or streamline? How might simplifying your environment, schedule, or thought processes contribute to your overall well-being and sense of peace? Experiment with implementing these strategies to see how they impact your mindset and daily experience.

39.
CARRY TWO OPPOSITES

You are capable to carry two opposing ideas in your mind. There are many such ideas. For example, take your best friend. You know the good sides and the bad sides. And still the friendship prevails.

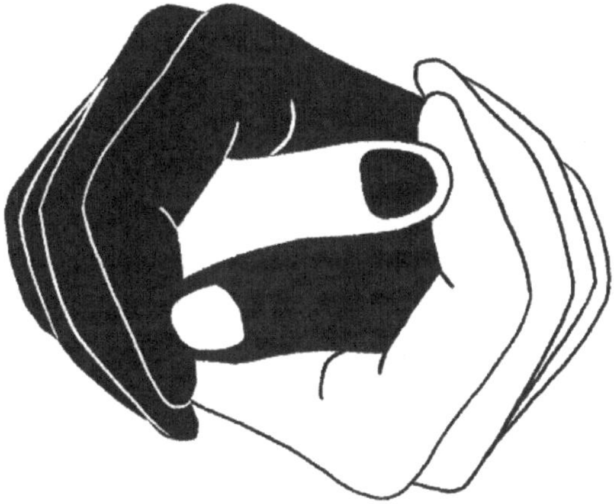

This applies to many areas of life. The mind feels the urge to pick one side and label things for the sake of false simplicity. Life is much too intricate and complex. To expand the mind, this skill has to be warmly welcome and nurtured. Carry two opposing ideas in your mind.

This keeps your eyes open to possibilities. Your awareness about the changing world will grow. You remain open to change and ready to adapt. This is a trait of an athletic mind, ready to jump when balance goes off.

This is also a necessary trait to keep everyone around, free to change their minds and evolve. Living things change. Business environment changes. The world changes. Fixed ideas about anything may hold you tightly at a position. Being open from strict opinion is liberating. As they say, **"Hold your strong opinions softly."**

One more thing, be slow with putting labels on everything. Life is meant to lived without labels. Use labels for convenience. And know clearly that labels do not explain in details. The content inside the label can change with time. Free your mind!

Exercises:

1. Perspective Switch: Choose a topic or situation that you have strong opinions about. Write down your current perspective on one side of a piece of paper. Then, on the other side, write down the opposite perspective or viewpoint. Spend some time exploring both sides, considering the arguments, emotions, and experiences associated with each perspective. This exercise can help you develop empathy, critical thinking skills, and the ability to hold opposing ideas in your mind simultaneously.

2. Role Reversal: Think of a scenario where you've had a disagreement or conflict with someone. Imagine yourself in the other person's shoes, trying to understand their perspective, motivations, and emotions. Write a letter or journal entry from their point of view, expressing their thoughts and feelings about the situation. This exercise can foster empathy, communication skills, and a more nuanced understanding of interpersonal dynamics.

Questions to Ponder:

1. How Does Holding Two Opposing Ideas Benefit Your Growth? Reflect on times when you've been able to entertain conflicting ideas or perspectives. How has this openness influenced your ability to learn, adapt, and grow? In what ways has it enhanced your relationships, decision-making process, or overall worldview?

2. What Challenges Do You Face in Holding Opposing Ideas? Consider any barriers or resistance you might encounter when trying to embrace contradictory viewpoints. Are there certain beliefs, biases, or fears that prevent you from fully engaging with opposing ideas? How might you overcome these challenges and cultivate a more open-minded approach to navigating complexity and uncertainty?

40.
FEAR FEAR

Why try to control fear when you can quit allowing fear to control you?

Fear has a purpose; it is your basic instinct telling you to avoid doing something. It's a poorly understood concept. Fear is actually a friend, but we frequently label it as the enemy.

In simple terms, don't be afraid of fear. It is healthy for you, we experience this emotion because it's programmed within our neurological system. Fear shares the same good intentions as a worried parent who doesn't want their child to suffer.

Embrace your fear as a friend, not an enemy, as the first step towards dealing with it. Fear is the messenger alerting us of the real threat; fear is not the threat. Because without it, we would lack an essential "survival instinct,".

I've come across all these "How to fight your fears" labeled articles and blogs online. And frankly, it's pointless. YOU DON'T HAVE TO FIGHT YOUR FEARS, that's not the answer. There's got to be a logical reason as to why we feel this emotion in the first place.

Accept your fear because it's looking out for you. And when you start doing that, you'll find the answers to your problems.

When you do something important in your life, you fear. If you did absolutely nothing, and I quite literally mean it, absolutely nothing, then you wouldn't experience these emotions.

Sadhguru once said something, and it stuck with me, he said, **"Enjoy the fear. After all, it's your making."**

Exercises:

1. Fear Journaling: Set aside some time each day to journal about your fears. Write down any fears or anxieties you're currently experiencing, along with the thoughts and emotions associated with them. Then, reflect on each fear individually and consider why it might be arising. Are there any underlying beliefs or past experiences contributing to these fears? This exercise can help you gain clarity and perspective on your fears, allowing you to approach them with greater understanding and acceptance.

2. Fear Exposure: Identify one fear that you've been avoiding or struggling with. Instead of trying to fight or suppress this fear, deliberately expose yourself to it in a controlled way. Start with small steps or manageable scenarios related to your fear, gradually increasing exposure over time as you become more comfortable. Notice how your feelings and reactions change as you confront your fear head-on. This exercise can help desensitize you to the fear and empower you to overcome it.

Questions to Ponder:

1. How Does Embracing Fear as a Friend Shift Your Perspective? Reflect on times when you've viewed fear as an enemy versus times when you've embraced it as a natural part of life. How does embracing fear as a friend change the way you respond to challenging situations? In what ways does it empower you to take action and move forward despite feeling afraid?

2. What Insights Can You Gain from Understanding the Purpose of Fear? Consider the evolutionary and psychological reasons behind the experience of fear. How

does understanding the purpose of fear help you navigate life's uncertainties and dangers more effectively? How can you use fear as a tool for growth and self-awareness rather than allowing it to hold you back?

41.
WHO IS YOUR PRIORITY

As you start looking deeper within, a few things will start to appear clearly. One of them is worth indicating here. Think about this one.

You are always doing things to decorate your image in the minds of others. That is how you have seen things from childhood, and maybe it is a social structure to keep things a little saner.

Let's zoom in on “others”. Who are these others? The obvious response from the mind would be the people around. But there is a twist in this story.

The one you call “yourself” could be the first “other”. Yes, strange, but worth looking into. This “other” is past-you and future-you. All your actions in the present are related to these two persons. There are many things you end up doing because of the past-you always thought of doing them. Likewise, there are many things your future-you wants you to do in order to reach that perfect future.

All the morals and ethics and codes of conduct and etiquette are not just for outer others, but also the inner “others”.

The question here is, who is your priority? Do you do things to look good in the eyes of others first, and then yourself? Or do you think it should be the opposite?

Happiness is making all your versions happy. Past - Present and Future. With the actions that you undertake in the present moment.

Most of the time, trying to impress others, you are hurting yourself, and you don't even apologize to yourself. This might have been a growing baggage on your mind. The remedy is a closed-door meeting with the "self".

And like me, if you have long neglected your very own self for the wellbeing of others, think on it. And yes, sincerely apologize to the self within. There is a lot more peace waiting for you after this little and harmless gesture.

You might want to experiment and decide your priority based on your life situation and experiences.

Exercises:

1. Self-Reflection Journaling: Set aside some time each day to reflect on your actions and decisions. Write down instances where you prioritized others over yourself, and vice versa. Explore the motivations behind these choices and how they made you feel. Then, brainstorm ways you can better align your priorities to include yourself in the equation. This exercise can help you become more aware of your habitual patterns and make intentional changes to prioritize your own well-being.

2. Future Self Visualization: Find a quiet space where you can relax and focus your mind. Close your eyes and visualize your future self – the person you aspire to become. Imagine this future version of yourself looking back on your current actions and decisions. Consider whether your present actions are serving the best interests of your future self or hindering your progress. Use this visualization as

motivation to prioritize actions that align with your long-term goals and aspirations.

Questions to Ponder:

1. Who Benefits Most from Your Actions: Others or Yourself? Reflect on the ways in which your actions and decisions impact both others and yourself. Are you primarily focused on pleasing and impressing others, or do you prioritize your own happiness and well-being? How might shifting your priorities towards self-care and self-fulfillment positively impact your overall satisfaction and fulfillment in life?

2. How Can You Strike a Balance Between Selflessness and Self-Care? Consider the importance of balancing your responsibilities and obligations to others with your own needs and desires. Are there areas of your life where you tend to overextend yourself in order to please others? How can you establish healthy boundaries and allocate time and energy for self-care without neglecting your relationships and commitments to others?

42.
FIVE MAGICAL SENSES

The self, as we know, is made of body and mind. We enjoy talking about mind, because it sounds very intellectual, but we forget about the body, which is our vehicle from birth to the end of this life. The body consists of five magical senses, which make us interact with the world and help us become who we are and make sense out of everything that happens inside and out. In the race to transform ourselves, our competition is the people outside, and we do what they do in order to defeat or control them. The utmost important and urgent need is to cleanse and expand the range of the senses by giving proper attention and care.

The five senses are sight, hearing, smell, taste, and touch. Each sense has its own unique function and purpose. Sight allows us to see the world around us. Hearing allows us to hear the sounds of the world. Smell allows us to detect different scents. Taste allows us to experience different flavors. Touch allows us to feel different textures.

The senses are not just passive receptors of information. They are also active participants in our experience of the world. When we see something, our brain interprets the image and creates a mental representation of it. When we hear something, our brain decodes the sound waves and creates a mental representation of the sound. When we smell something, our brain identifies the chemicals in the air and creates a mental representation of the smell. When we taste something, our brain identifies the different flavors and creates a mental representation of the taste. When we touch something, our brain interprets the pressure and temperature of the object and creates a mental representation of the touch.

The senses are essential for our survival. They allow us to perceive the world around us and make decisions about how to interact with it. They also allow us to experience the world in all its richness and beauty.

In the race to transform ourselves, we often focus on our mind and neglect our body. We try to control our thoughts and emotions, but we forget that our body is the foundation of our mind. When we neglect our body, we are neglecting our mind. The body is a complex and delicate system. It needs proper care and attention in order to function at its best. We need to eat healthy foods, get enough sleep, and exercise regularly. We also need to take care of our mental health by managing stress, practicing relaxation techniques, and getting professional help if needed.

When we take care of our body, we are taking care of our mind. We are giving our mind the foundation it needs to function at its best. We are also giving ourselves the opportunity to experience the world in all its richness and beauty.

Here are some to-do pointers on how to cleanse and expand the range of the senses:

- Sight: Spend time in nature. Look at the trees, the flowers, the animals. Take a walk in the park. Go for a hike in the woods.
- Hearing: Listen to music. Go to a concert. Listen to the birds singing. Listen to the waves crashing on the shore.
- Smell: Take a walk through a flower garden. Light a scented candle. Cook a delicious meal.
- Taste: Eat a variety of foods. Try new flavors. Experiment with different cooking techniques.
- Touch: Take a warm bath. Get a massage. Go for a walk barefoot.

When you take the time to cleanse and expand the range of your senses, you are opening yourself up to a whole new world of experience. You are also giving yourself the opportunity to grow and evolve as a person.

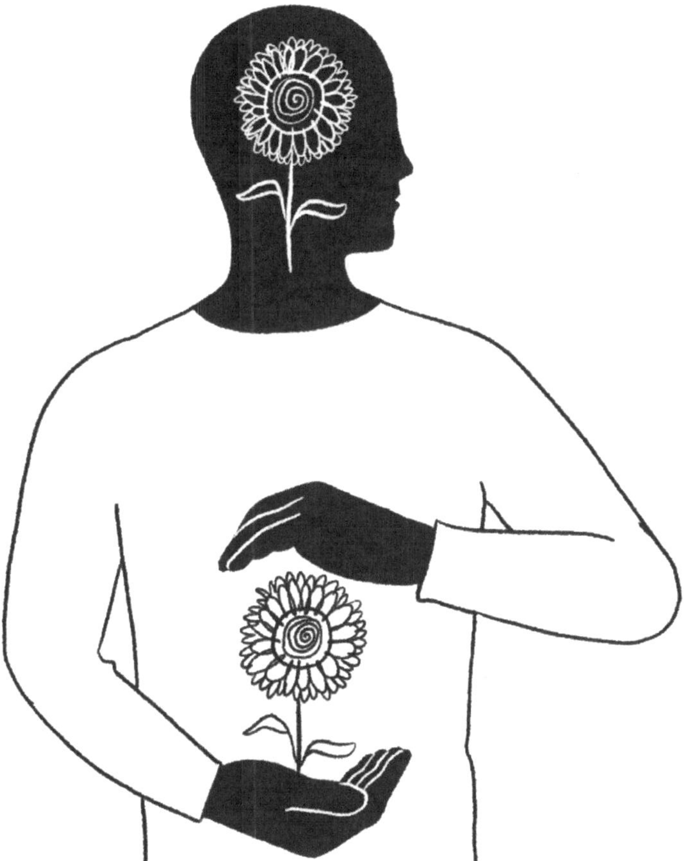

Exercises:

1. Sensory Awareness Meditation: Find a quiet and comfortable space where you won't be disturbed. Close your eyes and take a few deep breaths to center yourself. Begin to focus on each of your senses one by one. Start with sight – visualize a peaceful scene or image in your mind's eye. Then, shift your focus to hearing – listen to the sounds around you, both near and far. Next, bring your attention to smell – notice any scents in the air, pleasant or otherwise. Move on to taste – become aware of any lingering flavors in your mouth or the sensation of hunger or thirst. Finally, concentrate on touch – feel the texture of your clothing against your skin or the surface you're sitting or lying on. Spend a few moments with each sense, allowing yourself to fully experience the present moment.

2. Sensory Exploration Walk: Take a leisurely walk outdoors, preferably in a natural setting like a park or forest. As you walk, pay close attention to each of your senses. Notice the vibrant colors and intricate details of the scenery around you (sight). Listen to the various sounds of nature, such as birds chirping, leaves rustling, or water flowing (hearing). Take deep breaths and inhale the fresh air, picking up on any scents carried by the breeze (smell). If possible, pluck a leaf or flower and gently crush it between your fingers to release its aroma. Along your walk, stop to sample different foods or beverages, savoring the flavors and textures (taste). Finally, reach out and touch the natural elements around you – the rough bark of a tree, the soft petals of a flower, or the cool water of a stream (touch). Allow yourself to fully immerse in the sensory experience of your surroundings.

Questions to Ponder:

1. How Often Do You Engage Your Senses Mindfully? Reflect on your daily routine and consider how often you consciously engage with each of your senses. Are you primarily focused on completing tasks and responsibilities, or do you make time to appreciate the sensory experiences available to you throughout the day? How might incorporating more mindfulness into your daily activities enhance your overall well-being and enjoyment of life?

2. What Sensory Experiences Bring You Joy and Fulfillment? Think about the sensory experiences that bring you the most joy, relaxation, or inspiration. Is it the sight of a beautiful sunset, the sound of laughter, the aroma of freshly baked cookies, the taste of your favorite meal, or the feeling of warm sunshine on your skin? How can you incorporate more of these experiences into your daily life to nourish your body and mind?

43.
THIS IS IT!

Everything is perfect. Even your desire to improve things within you and the world outside too is part of this perfection.

All the events are happening because nature has designed them that way. The people you come across in your life are for invisible reasons. It is all for your growth, your evolution, and constant learning.

Just give your undivided attention to what is in front of you. Nothing is unimportant. This understanding will deepen, and it will bring light to your everyday life. And yes, the most important thing is the one happening right now. Yes, seriously!

Even your imagination about the past and future happening in the present moment is important. Just try not to change things too harshly. It is all happening for good reasons, as nature knows the best. Just practice observing things inside your mind. Observe the resistance to this recommendation I am giving. I know what you are feeling because I have gone through it.

Everything anyone can teach you is conceptual. You will have to create your inner world brick by brick.

This will happen organically as a tree grows. Just look back five or ten years behind. Chances are, you may feel amazed at how life changed. You might see that there is very little to do with what you did as a doer of things. And a lot more has to do with how everything happened naturally.

Paying sincere attention to what is happening at this moment is pure meditation. Taking note and following it up as per the system we created will grow over time. You will have a far-evolved system in years to come, and probably you too will share it with others like I am doing.

Always remember that,
There is perfection in the present moment!

You will find yourself arriving when the meaning of these words becomes clear. All in good time!

Exercises:

1. Present Moment Observation: Take a few moments to sit in a quiet space and bring your attention fully to the present moment. Notice the sensations in your body – the feeling of your feet on the ground, the rhythm of your breath, the temperature of the air against your skin. Then, expand your awareness to your surroundings – the sounds you hear, the colors and shapes you see, any scents in the air. Allow yourself to fully immerse in the experience of being present without judgment or analysis. Practice returning to this state of presence whenever you notice your mind wandering.

2. Gratitude Journaling: Set aside some time each day to reflect on the things you're grateful for in your life. Write down three to five things that you appreciate, whether big or small. They could be moments of joy, acts of kindness from others, or simply the beauty of nature around you. As you write, take a moment to truly feel the gratitude in your heart for these blessings. Over time, this practice can help shift your focus towards the abundance and perfection of the present moment.

Questions to Ponder:

1. How Do You Feel When You Fully Embrace the Present Moment? Reflect on your experiences of being fully present and observe how it affects your state of mind and emotions. Do you feel more calm, centered, and at peace? How does being present enhance your ability to appreciate the beauty and wonder of life as it unfolds moment by moment?

2. What Resistance Do You Encounter When Trying to Embrace the Present Moment? Consider any obstacles or challenges that arise when you attempt to fully immerse yourself in the present moment. Are there distractions, worries, or preoccupations that pull your attention away from the here and now? How can you cultivate greater awareness and acceptance of these inner and outer distractions in order to deepen your connection to the present moment?

44.
WHO IS WATCHING

You have a mind. And this book is about understanding the splits in the mind. There is one observation you will come across on this path at its own time. As you keep going deeper in this process, the deeper layers will appear. And then a striking revelation of the one who is watching the whole show.

It is tempting to put a label on this watcher. Maybe a part of mind is a comfortable label. Maybe it actually is a part of the mind. Maybe, it is not the mind at all.

Mind is the one which takes sides. It has opinions. The one which has no opinion is a plain watcher. And because it is a plain watcher, it can see things in true light without any colored shades.

This state will not stay longer in the beginning because being opinionated is a comfort zone for most of us. And this state of beyond label is discomforting in the beginning. So we tend to fall down to the old tendency of labeled city of mind.

But the taste of land beyond right and wrong is delicious. And you will return to it even if mind has any opinion against it.

The one who is watching is the point of reference for mind. It is a cue for the mind to start slowing down because there is less to process.

Exercises:

1. Witnessing Meditation: Set aside a few minutes for a simple meditation practice focused on witnessing. Find a comfortable seated position, close your eyes, and bring your attention to your breath. As you breathe in and out, observe the thoughts, emotions, and sensations that arise in your mind and body without getting caught up in them. Imagine yourself as the silent observer, simply witnessing everything that arises without judgment or attachment. Practice returning to this state of witnessing whenever you notice yourself becoming identified with your thoughts or emotions.

2. Journaling Reflection: Take some time to reflect on your experiences of witnessing throughout the day. Write down moments when you noticed yourself stepping back from your thoughts and simply observing. Describe how it felt to adopt this perspective and any insights or revelations that arose from it. Consider how you can cultivate more moments of witnessing in your daily life and the potential benefits it may bring to your overall well-being.

Questions to Ponder:

1. Who or What is the "Watcher" in Your Experience? Reflect on your understanding of the observer or "watcher" within yourself. Is it a distinct entity separate from your thoughts and emotions, or is it an aspect of your consciousness that transcends the mind? How does recognizing this aspect of yourself impact your perception of reality and your ability to navigate life's challenges with clarity and insight?

2. How Can You Cultivate a Greater Connection to the Witnessing Presence? Consider practical strategies for deepening your connection to the state of witnessing in

your everyday life. What practices or habits can you incorporate into your routine to nurture this aspect of yourself? How might cultivating a sense of detachment from your thoughts and emotions enhance your overall sense of peace, freedom, and self-awareness?

45. MIND MAPPING FOR CLARITY

In today's fast-paced world, the ability to think clearly and decisively is a valuable skill. Amidst the chaos of information overload and constant distractions, finding clarity of thought can seem like an elusive goal.

However, there exists a powerful tool that can help us organize our thoughts, visualize complex ideas, and unlock the full potential of our minds: mind mapping. The Essence of an How

To not to be your own enemy? : To truly harness the power of our minds, it is essential to cultivate an undivided focus.

When our thoughts are scattered and fragmented, it becomes challenging to grasp the big picture or make meaningful connections. Mind mapping offers a solution by providing a structured framework for organizing our thoughts around a central idea.

The Art of Thinking: At the heart of effective thinking lies the ability to synthesize information, make connections, and generate insights. Mind mapping serves as a catalyst for this process by allowing us to visually represent our thoughts and ideas.

By placing the central idea in the center of a page and branching out to explore various aspects and elements, we gain a comprehensive understanding of the subject at hand. **Clarity in Complexity:** One of the most significant benefits of mind mapping is its ability to distill complexity into simplicity. By breaking down complex concepts into manageable chunks and visualizing the relationships between them, we can navigate even the most intricate subjects with ease.

Whether brainstorming new ideas, outlining projects, or studying for exams, mind mapping provides a clear roadmap for success. **Embracing Contradictions:** In the realm of mind mapping, contradictions are not obstacles but opportunities for exploration. By embracing divergent viewpoints and conflicting ideas, we open ourselves up to new perspectives and creative solutions.

The ability to accommodate opposing viewpoints on the same page fosters a holistic understanding of the topic and encourages critical thinking. **Beyond Pen and Paper:** While mind mapping traditionally involves putting pen to paper, the principles behind it can be applied to various aspects of life. Whether brainstorming ideas, planning projects, or solving problems, the mind mapping approach encourages us to think expansively and make connections across different domains.

With practice, mind mapping becomes not just a tool but a way of thinking—one that promotes clarity, creativity, and innovation. Conclusion: In a world inundated with information and distractions, the ability to think clearly and critically is more valuable than ever. Mind mapping offers a simple yet powerful method for organizing our thoughts, visualizing complex ideas, and unlocking our full cognitive potential.
By embracing the principles of mind mapping, we can cultivate an How To Be Your Own Best Friend? capable of navigating the complexities of the modern world with clarity and confidence.

Exercises:

1. https://www.udemy.com/course/the-secrets-of-effective-mind-mapping/
   Udemy Course: Step-by-Step Mind Mapping: SMART Productivity and Memory Tool
   Author: Barry Mapp

2. Mind Mapping Practice: Choose a topic or problem you'd like to explore, whether it's a personal goal, a project at work, or a concept you're trying to understand better. Take a blank piece of paper or use a digital mind mapping tool and place the central idea or question in the center. Then, branch out from the central idea, adding subtopics, ideas, or questions related to it. Use colors, symbols, and images to enhance your map and make connections between different elements. Spend some time exploring the

relationships between the various components of your mind map and refining your understanding of the topic.

3. Reflective Mind Mapping: Take a moment to reflect on your recent experiences, thoughts, and emotions. Consider creating a mind map to visually represent the different aspects of your inner world. Start with a central node labeled "My Inner World" and branch out to explore different thoughts, feelings, and experiences you've had recently. Use the mind map as a tool for self-reflection and introspection, identifying patterns, insights, and areas for growth. Allow yourself to embrace contradictions and conflicting emotions, acknowledging that they are all part of the complex tapestry of your inner life.

Questions to Ponder:

1. How Does Mind Mapping Enhance Clarity of Thought? Reflect on your experience with mind mapping and consider how it helps you organize your thoughts, make connections between ideas, and gain a clearer understanding of complex subjects. How does visualizing your thoughts in a mind map format contribute to your ability to think critically and creatively?

2. What Role Does Embracing Contradictions Play in Mind Mapping? Explore the idea of embracing contradictions and conflicting viewpoints within the context of mind mapping. How does allowing for divergent perspectives enhance your ability to explore complex topics and generate innovative solutions? In what ways does the inclusive nature of mind mapping encourage open-mindedness and creativity?

46.
WRITE WHAT YOU LEARN.

As you arrive at the end of a small journey here, I will leave you with one suggestion that took a long time to pop up 💡 in my head.

Reading is a popular hobby for a few reasons. One reason is, everyone says it is great to read. Tell me honestly, what do you think? I mean, yes reading has many advantages and all but only if you follow a system. Just reading for the sake of reading is like a warm shower. Feels good while it lasts, but after it is over, there's nothing!

My point is, read to absorb the ideas worth absorbing. Write what you grasped from the book. This will prime the mind with a nitro booster. Imagine you are going to write a book of your own after reading a few books on a single subject. In that case, you could become a mini google on that subject, not?

The satisfaction of such quality reading is priceless. And it is possible that you will start enjoying the process of Learning = Reading + Writing.

You can write in the side spaces of the book or a large sticky note which you can stick inside the book. You can create digital notes in any free note-taking app.

"Just Reading is incomplete. While reading, start writing ✍ what you understood from the book 📖. If you're lazy, at least start talking and 🎙 recording."

The point is, your energy is precious, and you want to carefully invest it in everything you enjoy doing. Learning is the only thing that has made our specie rule this planet (...most of it, I mean!) And this is the only thing that can make you the ruler of your inner world.

This book too is a product of my learning system, which I developed over many years. It is evolving every day. It is ready enough to a stage that I don't want you to reinvent the wheel. I am passing it on to you and someday you too will do the same.

All the best!

Exercises:

1. Read and Reflect: Choose a book or an article on a topic that interests you. As you read, actively engage with the material by jotting down key points, insights, and questions that arise. After finishing the reading, take some time to reflect on what you've learned and write a brief summary or reflection on the main ideas. Consider how the information applies to your own life or work and what actions you can take based on your new knowledge.

2. Create a Learning Journal: Start a learning journal where you document your reading and writing journey. Each time you finish a book or article, write a short entry summarizing the main ideas, your thoughts, and any personal connections you made. Over time, you'll build a valuable record of your intellectual growth and insights. Reviewing your journal periodically can also help you track your progress and identify areas for further exploration.

Questions to Ponder:

1. How Does Writing Enhance the Learning Process? Reflect on your experience with writing about what you've learned from reading. How does the act of writing help you better understand and internalize the material? In what ways does writing facilitate deeper engagement with the content and retention of key concepts?

2. What Role Does Active Engagement Play in Learning? Consider the difference between passive reading and active engagement with the material. How does actively writing about what you've read enhance your comprehension, critical thinking skills, and overall learning experience? How can you incorporate more active learning strategies into your daily routine to maximize your growth and development?